THE CAPTIVE
MUSE

On Creativity and Its Inhibition

SUSAN KOLODNY

Psychosocial Press
Madison, Connecticut

Library of Congress Cataloging-in-Publication Data

Kolodny, Susan.
    The captive muse : on creativity and its inhibition / Susan Kolodny.
      p. cm.
    Includes bibliographical references and index.
    ISBN 1-887841-27-X
     1. Creation (Literary, artistic, etc.) I. Title.

BF408.K65 1999
153.3'5—dc21

                                       99-047269

Manufactured in the United States of America

For Lewis, who shared bed and table with this book.
For Noah, may he never need this book.
And for he who met the muse unafraid.

CONTENTS

ACKNOWLEDGMENTS

The author gratefully acknowledges:

My patients, for all they have taught me and for helping to make this book, a by-product of our work together, possible.

The six artists who granted the interviews, for their generosity, candor, and insight.

My teachers in both worlds, and all who made possible my experiences in the Doctorate in Mental Health Program; the Department of Psychiatry, Mount Zion Hospital and Medical Center; and the M.F.A. Program for Writers at Warren Wilson College. Special thanks to Calvin Settlage for his generous, helpful comments, theoretical and editorial, about chapter 6. Special thanks also, and always, to Brooks Haxton, Brigit Pegeen Kelly, Ira Sadoff, and Renate Wood.

The Community of Writers, particularly Alan Williamson, who encouraged me to expand an essay I had written into this book and offered useful comments about the creative process, and Helen Fremont, for her friendship, generosity, astute editorial help, and support, in cyberspace and beyond.

Martha Rabkin, for her friendship, her interest in this project, and the sage editorial suggestions she offered, along with Norman Rabkin.

Alice Jones and Forrest Hamer, poet friends and clinical colleagues, for conversations that supported and helped to inform this book; and poet friend, Carol Snow, for those walks, with koans.

That friend and poetry mentor who asked not to be named but is here acknowledged, nonetheless, and loved.

She who helped make the writing possible again.

Margaret Emery, Editor-in-Chief of Psychosocial Press, who knew exactly when to advise and how much.

Cindy Lobel and Rita Barrera of *Mouse Bytes*, San Francisco, whose technical support with computer and printer, like their patience and good humor, has been beyond the call.

The editors of *AWP Chronicle, A Publication of the Associated Writing Programs*, and *Fort Da, The Journal of the Northern California Society for Psychoanalysis and Psychotherapy*, in which sections of this book first appeared.

Character is fate. (Heraclitus)

What you love is your fate. (Bidart, 1990)

INTRODUCTION

Nineteen years ago, I attended a Fourth of July party where, uninterested in the conversations going on around me, I wandered into the dining room in search of other sustenance. A woman who joined me there caught my attention when, without looking up from the buffet, she asked drolly if I, too, were retreating to the canapes. We began to talk. I learned she was a poet. My questions about her and her work made her ask if I wrote also. I told her I was a psychotherapist who used to write fiction and poetry, but had been blocked for years. Then something—the intimacy which developed between us as we spoke of writing, an urgency that I'd forgotten until that moment was in me—made me cry out, "*Why* is writing so difficult?" "It *is* difficult," she said. With that, a friendship began and, though I wasn't to know it for more than a decade and a half, this book did also.

A few years after the conversation over the canapes, and with the help of psychoanalysis, I resumed writing. I began to get poems published and, as others learned of my dual life as therapist and poet, to see more artists and writers in psychotherapy. I realized as I became a more disciplined writer and as I listened to patients who worked seriously in the arts, that what I'd previously experienced hadn't necessarily been writer's block. Some would have considered it instead to be a failure, born of fear, even to sit down and try. Yet writer's block—or painter's block, or musician's block, because this isn't, after all, only about writing—may begin with exactly such periodic or chronic avoidance of studio or desk. It may begin with an inability, once there and trying, to produce anything we can bear to look at, or with a failure to produce work consistent with the highest expectations that we have for ourselves, reasonably or unreasonably, *though we steadily try.* Whichever of these we suffer from, if we believe ourselves to be blocked and become so, then the distress we will feel, the alienation from an important part of the self, will be considerable. The questions to be asked will be compelling, and the answers important to find.

I wrote this book as a way of grappling with questions which had long plagued me. *Why* is creative work so difficult? Why, when we've made time to write, do we struggle with a sudden temptation to do laundry? Why are there poems or stories, or for that matter, dissertations and professional papers, that seem tenaciously to resist us, or present themselves as if the oracle were speaking, then stubbornly defy our attempts at revision? Why is there writer's block? Why do visual artists often encounter difficulties as they approach paper, canvas, or stone, find themselves doing the same thing over and over, or get little done despite the wish to accomplish much?

In time my questions coalesced, then evolved, into three, and it is these that I will attempt to answer: (1) Why is creative work often so difficult? (2) What helps and what hinders us in doing it? (3) What makes such work possible? Two clarifications, apropos of question 1, are called for here: My concern is with difficulties from within and not those imposed by external circumstances, though as we will see, what appears to be externally imposed is often chosen by us or allowed to interfere. I don't mean to suggest that creative work *ought* to be easy. That which confronts us with charged emotional material and so mobilizes our anxiety in response is inevitably difficult. Tension must build within the artist if creative work is to be done, and a need to face that tension or anxiety, to take on that difficulty, can help to motivate creative work, while the anxiety, transmuted, is often one source of the work's power. But for many, the difficulty which is inherent in the work is compounded by internal conflicts or inhibitions, and though I will consider the anxieties which are inevitable in creative work, it is primarily the compounded versions that I will attempt to explain.

I come to my subject as a former college English teacher who taught remedial writing, composition, and literature, and as a poet, sometimes productive and sometimes not. I come to my subject also as a psychotherapist, trained in psychoanalytic theory and therapy, who, in 23 years of clinical practice, has worked with a number of writers and visual artists. These experiences, particularly as a therapist, but also as a poet, incline me to look to psychoanalytic theory and practice for ways to understand the writer's, or indeed any creative person's process. Certainly the therapy that proceeds from analytic theory has elements in common with creative work. Both, to borrow from T. S. Eliot's *Four Quartets* (1944/1958), are "raid(s) on the inarticulate." Both are processes and so require time and patience; they cannot by-pass but must instead come to terms with the obstacles they encounter. Both confront us with charged emotional material and so mobilize anxiety. What might psychoanalytic theory and therapy tell us about the difficulties encountered in creative work? (The reader interested in a review of the pertinent analytic literature is referred to Leader [1991], as well as to the other sources cited throughout this book.)

I begin with a basic psychoanalytic concept. I suggest that much of the difficulty we encounter when we try to write or do other creative work, is a result of *resistance* (a.k.a. defense), mobilized, as resistances are, because we feel, consciously or unconsciously, that in proceeding, we place ourselves in danger. Again, a clarification: In discussing resistance, I don't mean to confuse the silences it may cause, or the sense of stuckness, with those fertile or gestative silences which are a necessary part of the creative process. It is not, of course, always clear to the artist (or to the therapist who may be working with the artist) which kind of silence pertains.

What elicits such resistance? In chapter 1, I show that it is some-times our feelings about the known or yet unknown *content* of the work. The content can feel dangerous because we fear what it will reveal. We may worry that the content will threaten our view of ourselves or the view which others have of us, confront us with our own emptiness, repeat past traumas, or damage our relationships.

Creative work can have problematic *unconscious meanings* for us, and these too can bring about resistance. I give examples in chapter 2. The work may affirm our separateness, and for some, this is itself a danger. The process may be felt to erase that separateness and so threaten to swallow us up. Creativity may be associated with prohibited erotic, aggressive, exhibitionistic, or competitive feelings, or seem to proclaim a dangerous triumph, putting us and our human connections in jeopardy.

Some of the difficulties we especially encounter when we revise, as I point out in chapter 3, are related to what psychoanalytic theory calls *character* or characteristic *defense style:* In revising, we come up against ourselves. Though my emphasis here is on writers revising, my examples apply to other creative work and perhaps to profes-sional work as well. If we typically can't allow ourselves to reveal what is true, or to tolerate ambiguity or ambivalence, what we create will reflect and share these limitations. So will it reflect what in us is rigid or flexible, needs to be absolutely in control or can be inventive and playful, needs to remain shallow, or is capable of richness and depth. I give examples of such parallels between character and the limita-tions of the work and show that the processes of changing the work and changing the self are intertwined.

We may, as I discuss in chapter 4, resist the momentary *regres-sions* which creative work often requires. Regression is that fluid, usually transient movement backwards in psychological develop-ment, in ways of thinking or perceiving, in the pleasures we seek or the fears we experience, and in how we defend ourselves. To give in to regression in the ways that creative work requires is to temporarily relinquish conscious, rational control over the workings of the mind. If we fear this, we will be unable to allow those mental processes and emotional states associated with inspiration and with creative or intuitive leaps to take over. We may especially be threatened by and resist the power of language and rhythm to evoke parental presences. This is a power that can serve us well at times of trauma, enrich our lives, and enhance our pleasure in the arts, but it can also increase our resistance to creative work.

In chapter 5, I describe a miscellany of other resistances. I consider what happens when, consciously or unconsciously, we attribute to real or imagined others reactions we associate with important people from our past. Such transferences, if negative, and to prospective readers, editors, judges, viewers, or critics, can cause us to fear and so avoid doing, showing, or submitting our work. Projection, which I touch on here, then elaborate on in chapter 7, can be similarly problematical. So can resistances which arise because of the strong feelings creative work may evoke in us, feelings we may avoid by avoiding specific details which embody or contain them. We may encounter resistance because we fear what we will reveal or expose; we may avoid starting because starting requires facing what is or isn't inside of us. Revision may be resisted, because it makes us face ourselves. To finish may be associated with closure or death. We may resist showing our work, accepting its limitations or strengths, or sending the work into the world where we relinquish control over it.

In chapter 6, I summarize the stages of psychological development and the challenges, tasks, and opportunities of each. How we negotiate these stages will have a significant impact on whether we are ultimately able to enjoy and to make art. Our relationship to feelings of omnipotence or helplessness, merger or separateness, to curiosity, to the products of our minds and bodies, to aggression, eroticism, exhibitionism, and competition, to our creative and procreative wishes and capacities, all contribute in important ways to whether we can take pleasure in and do creative work.

Those inner voices which plague or sustain artists and writers, and those "Watchers at the Gate" which try, sometimes ruthlessly, to keep the muse at bay, are the subject of chapter 7. I discuss these denizens of the inner world in relationship to internal objects and to the processes of internalization whereby such helpers or hinderers get set up within. Relevant here are the superego and other agencies of the inner world as these help or hinder. Relevant also is the important and complex nature of the artist's relationship to his or her art. To illustrate how intense and nuanced that relationship can be, I conclude the chapter by quoting, in their entirety, three contemporary poems.

The outer world, in the form of parents, teachers, and attitudes—toward creativity, conformity, what constitutes success, and who may create—helps to form, and then interacts with, the inner world. In chapter 8, I consider how such interactions as these influence the internal voices that sustain or undermine us. I comment on a tendency among some mental health professionals and others to pathologize those who do creative work, or to be unduly interested in the presumed psychopathology of the artist. I suggest that this is an expression of envy and can be damaging to those already in conflict or in doubt about their talent or their right to do their work.

Chapter 9 consists of excerpts from interviews I conducted with six unblocked, accomplished artists. The six speak candidly about what has helped them, what has sometimes gotten in their way, how their creativity was responded to in their childhood homes, what part teachers and friends have played for them, how they have coped with internal obstacles to their creativity, including their own inner voices and Watchers at the Gate. They discuss how they think about creative blocks, or feeling stuck, and describe the commitment and the joy that keep them going.

In chapter 10, I propose that the difficulties we encounter when we do creative work are of three orders. I discuss the apparent relationships of the interviewees to these and reflect on what in the six, besides talent, enables them to keep working. What aspects of their character or personality, as revealed in the interviews, have helped them, despite personal problems and inevitable frustrations? What implications do the interviews and the inferences which may be drawn from them have for those who wish to make art or to understand what enables some to do so?

I believe that this book will be of use to therapists and analysts, to blocked and unblocked writers and artists, to teachers of writing and art, and to those with a more general interest in creativity and in what nurtures this vital resource or gets in its way.

For therapists, this book offers ways of thinking about creative people which do *not* pathologize them. It offers an opportunity to hear, sometimes in artists' own words, what the creative process can mean to those involved in it, and what unhappiness can result from an inhibition of that process. It considers psychological conflicts and psychopathology as these restrict, constrict, or otherwise inhibit creativity, and *not* as inevitable to creative people, typical of them, or as what motivates the making of art. It offers therapists a chance to consider both their own feelings and assumptions about creativity, and those of people with whom they may work. This seems useful because if we don't understand the place in our patients' lives of their creativity, or if we have unrecognized envy of it, such limitations on our part can lead to significant failures of empathy, to destructiveness, or to impasse. The tendency to pathologize may be born of envy, ignorance, or misguided theories. Respect for our patients' creativity, empathy for and understanding of their struggles to develop and express it, and receptivity to the richness and importance of their experience and process, can only enhance the therapeutic encounter and its outcome, *for both participants.*

Writers and artists, and people wanting to write or make art, will find examples here of what gets in the way, with analyses of how it does and why. They will, I believe, be helped to better understand their own process, including what facilitates or frustrates it. To determine the nature of the obstacles we face, to get better acquainted with the process so we know what is simply a difficult but inevitable phase in it, may help some to face the canvas or the page. Others, and I suggest who they are, will find that such information, reflection, and practice, while interesting, do not suffice, and that psychotherapy or psychoanalysis (both of which can still sometimes be found at substantially reduced fees) may also be required.

Teachers of writing and art, the good ones, at least, understand a great deal about the creative process and what is called for during some of its more difficult phases. Nonetheless, I believe this book will offer them some useful ways of thinking about what goes on internally for their students and perhaps also for themselves when obstacles are encountered. This can help them to help their students understand more about the process, including those times when the muse seems to have packed up and left town.

Readers with a general interest in creativity, and perhaps especially parents of potential artists will, I hope, find here some ways to better understand what the creative process involves. What seems to foster and what to hinder its unfolding? What is living it like? What price do we pay whose muse is captive? What struggles and what joys does the work afford those who are free to do it? I hope that such readers will also find here some useful ways of considering what in their own reactions, in the ways they educate their children or allow them to be educated, and in the culture or the family itself may threaten their children's creativity or help to nurture it and keep it free.

WHEN THE RESISTANCE IS TO CONTENT

> [T]o think of resistance as the
> construction of an obstacle might lead us
> to redefine resistances as peculiarly
> inventive artifacts. (Phillips, 1993, p. 86)

I was trying, years ago, to finish a poem about a patient who had died of cancer. The poem was relatively satisfying; it had a certain vitality and horror; it acknowledged the young woman's courage, our respective forms of helplessness. But the ending, which was about her death, didn't work. That is to say, 20, 40 different drafts of the ending didn't work. I couldn't figure out what was wrong. I showed various versions to poet friends; they thought the ending bordered on the sentimental, though they liked the rest of the poem well enough. What was my problem in writing the ending? I focused on technique—played with line breaks, diction, worked on the closing image, experimented with the sounds. Nothing seemed to help until a mentor reminded me that "revision" is "re-vision," seeing it again. She said, "Go back into the experience."

When I tried to think about how I'd really felt about my patient's death, I had to admit that while I had tried repeatedly to convey sadness, grief, sympathy, and regret, the truth was that when she died, after months of my seeing her in hospitals, her home, the hospice, having to encounter her difficult family, feeling helpless but unwilling to abandon her as she had feared I would, my strongest feeling was relief. This being faced, I was able to finish the poem.

I might ultimately have been more satisfied had I considered my patient's death to be what Hugo has called a "triggering" event (1979, p. 4), and not treated it, in its specifics, as my subject matter. I might then have let myself see not only how I had really experienced her death, but also some of the bigger questions that the poem may have wanted to investigate, about the limits of my omnipotence, about my own mortality. I didn't investigate these questions, however, until a later poem about a different and closer death. Still, it proved helpful in the writing of this earlier poem, with all its limitations, to see what feelings about the triggering event, and about myself, I had been attempting to avoid.

The term *resistance* technically means the use, in the therapeutic context, of psychological mechanisms of "defense." When that part of the mind which decides what constitutes danger determines certain of our ideas, wishes, or feelings to be dangerous, it institutes defenses against these, censoring or distorting until such ideas, wishes, or feelings are less accessible to us. Such judgments are often made unconsciously and therefore are not subject to reason or reconsideration in the light of new information. Things that were dangerous once but aren't anymore, or that were never dangerous, but were imagined to be so, may still be treated as if they were dangerous now. This, of course, is what predisposes us to neurosis.

I consciously believe there was nothing wrong with my reaction to my patient's death. But something in me, presumably my ideas about the sort of person and therapist I am, considered my relief unacceptable, perhaps even dangerous, and made use of the defense mechanism we call denial, the one that says you don't feel or think or know something which in fact you do. I made use of other defenses in my poem. I tried to turn negative feelings into positive ones, selfish feelings into generous ones. I tried, that is, to avoid anxiety by distorting what I'd really felt. I did so to the poem's detriment because these distortions made the poem, or at least its conclusion, ring false. Similar defenses or resistances can crop up whenever we write and can stop us from writing or doing any kind of creative work at all.

When such resistances or defenses occur in psychotherapy or in psychoanalysis, and they do all the time, one has the means to make good use of them. One has, or is, a therapist; the therapist analyzes the resistances. As writers or artists, however, working on our own, we may not always know how or be able to do this, though there are strategies that can help. I will consider some of these later on.

Sometimes positive feelings are the hard ones to admit. I was working on a poem about a man I'd once been foolish enough to love; the relationship ended badly. While the poem was rather clever, a poem of revenge, a teacher pointed out that my revenge had backfired; I'd failed to show the attraction that accounted for the bitterness which the poem contained. I had to go back into the poem and the experience, to revise or re-see it, to get the attraction into the poem, as well as the anger and disdain. This made for a better poem in the end; earlier drafts were less successful because I hadn't been letting myself in on my own more complex experience—my resistance to acknowledging my own experience had been in my way.

There are examples from other genres, even other media, of how resistance may be mobilized in response to specific content. A friend of mine, an extraordinarily gifted therapist, had been studying painting for several years when she was diagnosed with breast cancer. At first, she thought painting would be a solace, a help to her in her battle with the disease. Then she looked at a painting she had done months before her diagnosis, a painting which had greatly frightened her at the time, though she hadn't understood why. The painting was of a shape which she realized in retrospect resembled a breast and within that shape, in the location where her malignancy had been, was a small, dark shadow. Her prescience, her having, she felt, been unconsciously aware of her illness, so frightened her that for months, she couldn't paint. She was too worried that she knew unconsciously she was going to die, and would somehow paint this and influence the outcome of her fight.

This woman was unusually attuned to her own and to other people's unconscious processes. Her fear about painting contained elements of both truth and superstition. And while this example is extreme, we all have moments of fearing what we will discover about ourselves.

In the examples I've given, what got in the way was the poet's or the painter's relationship to content, the content of the poem she needed to write or of the painting she feared but needed to paint. There seems often to be a fear that the work, like Rilke's *Archaic Torso . . .* , will see us too clearly and force us to confront ourselves. It does, of course, which is part of what makes the venture deeply satisfying. Each of us has the opportunity, in confronting a poem or painting, or perhaps a professional paper as well, to discover some truth about ourselves, and in the process, to strengthen whatever we have made.

This is also part of what makes creative work scary. We may not feel ready or able to confront the charged material, particularly since, when we set out, we probably don't even know what that material is, what unconscious wishes it may express, or meanings it may have for us. We may be daunted also by the anxiety that this mobilizes in us. If the anxiety is too intense, we may be tempted to turn away. Or, as psychoanalytic theory teaches us, the anxiety may not even be registered consciously; a little warning spurt of it can cause us to institute defenses automatically, so that suddenly, without knowing why, we are denying our feelings or ideas or shutting them down and turning elsewhere. The poem we are writing may go dead, the painting may become lifeless, the sculpture be left unfinished, the book manuscript put aside. The infamous "visitor from Porlock" who shattered Coleridge's vision during the writing of *Kubla Khan,* causing that poem to be left unfinished, may have been a person at the door, but could as easily have been a visitor from that part of the psyche which thinks danger is imminent and tries at whatever cost to protect us from it from within.

There are other examples of how resistance can be mobilized in response to emotionally charged content. A painter with whom I worked in therapy reported feeling dissatisfied with her need always to contain the objects within her paintings in a manner that seemed to her to have become rigid and limiting. When she tried not to frame or arrange them in this way, she became anxious and unable to proceed. As she described this experience, I asked what she imagined would happen if she didn't make use of her strategies for holding things carefully in place. Then, suddenly, I thought of the scene in the Kubrick film, *2001,* in which H.A.L., the computer, having discovered that the astronauts are about to shut him down, gets one of them to go outside the ship to do some repairs and while the astronaut is there, severs the support line that connects him to the mother ship, causing him to drift off helplessly into space.

What the patient then said suggested that I had, in my association, been attuned to her: She was afraid that if the "objects" she painted were not carefully contained, they'd all drift off in separate directions, unconnected and alone, as she had felt unconnected and alone as a child. Initially, when she used the word *objects,* she seemed to be talking about things, but I came to believe that though she was unfamiliar with psychoanalytic language and theory, she had somehow intuited that these "things" stood for objects in the analytic sense. They represented people to whom she was significantly connected and with whom she had "object ties." The things she painted and had to keep carefully corraled together also represented parts of herself which she feared would become, or be revealed to be, unconnected from the rest, and so either lost or destroyed.

As we explored this aspect of her art and its meanings to her, she began to experiment with paintings that didn't include the limiting or structuring pattern. What she noticed immediately, and what others seeing her work subsequently commented on, was that the various objects she painted when she didn't use her framing or bordering strategies did indeed seem to be floating in space. They were unrelated to each other and lonely, precisely as she was beginning to realize she had felt herself to be in relationship to important others in her childhood and they in relationship to her.

Milner (1957, ch. 2) has discussed exactly this aspect of painting. She has noted that the placement of various objects and the relationships the painter creates among these reflect important unconscious aspects of his or her "inner object world," including feelings of estrangement, fears of engulfment, and wishes for merger. If an artist needs to avoid experiencing these, as my patient did for a time, she may become blocked in her work or use certain patterns or forms defensively, even compulsively, thus restricting her creative growth.[1]

My patient and I began to explore the meanings of the unattached floating objects that appeared after she stopped using rigid patterns to keep things seemingly connected and contained. We were, as a result, better able to understand important aspects of her early relationships. She became aware of profound feelings of rejection and loss, resulting anger, and wishes for distance, fears that her wishes had irrevocably brought such distance about. She felt relieved by this work and excited to be able, in her art, to explore the lonely, sad feelings more freely and effectively for as long as she seemed to need to do so. Then she was able, excitedly, to move on, by experimenting in a way that apparently exhilarated her, with painting onto and over the picture frames. The limiting borders and boundaries had become helpfully containing, but not inevitably or rigidly so. They could now be breached experimentally, and when they served to contain, it was in a way that comforted but did not restrict, ordered but did not oppress.

During this same period in our work, she began to be able, in relationship to me, to express both critical thoughts and affectionate feelings. She was able to be curious about me as a person, to explore her worries about who I might really turn out to be if she let herself inquire. She could then consider how she had needed to keep such feelings, fantasies, and thoughts in relationship to me tightly contained, out of a similar concern that what wasn't so contained, within herself and her pictures, could lead to estrangement or loss.

This example, like my previous ones, involved resistance in response to anxiety about the anticipated or feared content of the work. This woman, however, feared the *relationships* among the things she depicted, worried what those relationships might reveal, and whether such revelations would prove painful or dangerous. Concerns with the relationships among the various elements or contents of a work aren't unique to the visual arts. They contribute also to the difficulty poets may have arranging the lines, stanzas, or sections of a poem, or arranging poems in a manuscript. I have heard poets talk with surprise about how rearranging a collection of poems can cause all the poems within it to change in response to what precedes or follows. Here, too, then, we have potentially complex meanings and feelings evoked by how the elements in a creative

---

[1] To avoid the stylistic clumsiness of repeatedly using "he or she," I have chosen to use "she" as the inclusive pronoun.

work may interact with each other, a variation on the theme of content and how it may mobilize resistance.

A poet I saw in therapy became anxious when her new, and to her, rather surprising work revealed parts of her that were neither suffering nor abject. Suffering and abjectness had previously been the only positions she felt she could assume if she were to remain connected to her deeply troubled family. It both excited and frightened her to allow what she called her "bad girl" or "smart ass voice" to come forth, as it seemed to be wanting to do, to allow herself to be playful, colorful, irreverent, or sexy. For a time she teetered between wanting to permit these parts of herself to emerge in her poems and in her life and wanting to suppress them. As we explored this conflict, it became clear that many aspects of herself, but especially the excited and alive ones, seemed dangerous to her because they appeared especially to threaten her tie to her depressed and self-destructive mother. As long as she wrote about and continued suffering, this important relationship did not seem in jeopardy, but her development as a person and an artist did. Hers is a story of which I don't know the outcome because this talented young woman insisted on leaving therapy abruptly at a point when material was emerging that appeared to offer her a wider range as a person and an artist.

Milner (1957, ch. 1) describes a related instance of resistance to content where the content was at odds with her sense of what parts of herself it was safe to experience or reveal. She did a series of stilted drawings when attempting to render beautiful scenes as beautiful, then tried "free drawings," letting her hand draw as it would. Only when she so freed herself of the expectation that what she would draw would portray what was beautiful (i.e., gave herself permission to discover her genuine responses to the scenes before her) did the drawings come alive. To allow them to do so, she had to risk discovering that beauty could elicit many feelings in her, including a sense of inner ugliness and terror, and this, she reports, she had been reluctant to do.

I worked with a professor who was on academic leave and struggling to turn her dissertation into the book she needed to publish in order to be granted tenure. It soon became apparent that her dissertation, which concerned female mentors and mentees, unconsciously represented to her the sexual and professional triumph of younger women over older ones. This woman's mother had been mentally ill during the patient's childhood and adolescence and had recently become significantly more so. (Interestingly, she had been better when the dissertation was being written, which may have enabled my patient to complete her Ph.D.) For her now to write her book, however, with her mother's condition worsening, to obtain tenure at a respected college as a result of that book, to succeed where her mother had consistently failed, and to do so on the basis of this particular subject matter, were possibilities she found immobilizing. It became clear even in our brief work that for her to succeed would have felt as if she were digging, then dancing on, her mother's grave. This she unconsciously longed to do, because her mother's difficulties had filled this woman's childhood with deprivations and disappointments. She longed also to protect and save her mother, which at first she felt only her own failure could accomplish. Though our work ended with her academic leave and her return to her campus in another state, she later let me know that she was continuing therapy there and making progress on her book. Our exploration of the meanings to her of the dissertation's symbolic content, as well as of what it meant to her to write her book and so get tenure, had helped free her to proceed, as the subsequent therapy was continuing to do.

I worked with a graduate student who came to me several years into the process of not writing his dissertation. His chosen topic, which concerned levels of psychopathology among men in his father's occupation, was intended to discredit his father, that occupation, which was closely related to his own, and his father's adequacy as a parent. Meanwhile, the prolonging of his graduate training was also prolonging his dependency on this same loved and maligned father. When we began, he was only slightly aware of what had motivated his choice of topics. What remained unconscious in his motivation contributed to his being stuck. Once we'd analyzed the meanings to him of his chosen topic, and the hostile feelings and intense dependency wishes that had motivated him to choose it but not get the work done, he began to be able to consider that, like many before him, he was having difficulty writing his thesis because of the highly conflictual meanings to him of getting a Ph.D. In other words, once one kind of resistance had been addressed, we were able to begin work on another.

Content may be resisted because it is associated with traumatic experience. We can hope that addressing such content in creative work, giving it form and shape, will enable us to distance ourselves from it and master the trauma. This may have happened for the authors of several fine books of poetry published in recent years on the Vietnam War and on childhood incest and sexual abuse. But we may fear that instead we will be flooded by and helpless in the face of the trauma once again. Whether we master or repeat the trauma when we do creative work with such material will depend on many things.

I was teaching a community college composition class during the last years of the Vietnam War. A young man in my class had failed to hand in several of his writing assignments. When I asked him why, he said he couldn't write, that when he tried, he became too distracted and upset. He said he thought he'd better drop my class. Then he told me that he'd recently come back from serving in Vietnam and that when he tried to write, he became flooded with horrible thoughts and images. He couldn't bear these and had to busy himself instead doing something mindless that would distract him. I was in no position then to help this man, who declined my offer of a referral to a therapist. He did, however, help me by giving me an early inkling of what it is about the blank page that can terrify many who face it. He was warding off intolerable content and the accompanying feelings, and clearly had no "holding environment" (Winnicott, 1965) in which he could be safely alone in the recalled, imagined, or felt presence of another. There was no setting in which, safely, to approach what was inside of him. The blank page offered him no prospect of relief, but rather the threat of being traumatized all over again.

A woman in the same class turned in a poignant essay about two experiences she later told me she hadn't, until then, been able to write about, reflect on, or describe. In both, she'd watched a man in military uniform approach her front door; in both, she had known immediately the nature of his errand. Each had come to tell her that her husband—her first, and then, a few years later, her second—had been killed in Vietnam. For *her*, facing the terrible content and giving it shape was not a repetition or exacerbation of a trauma, as writing seemed potentially to be for the veteran, but an opportunity instead to master one. This seemed clear from the intensely moving but also resolved way the paper was written, and from this woman's description of the relief she felt, the sense of closure she began to experience when she handed the paper in.

I know little about either student personally. I assume, though, years of clinical experience later, that not only the vastly different nature of their respective traumas, but also many personal traits and circumstances, allowed one to face the dreadful content and the other to need to hide from it. One was able finally to give the trauma shape by writing about it, and the other lived in terror of being swallowed up by it again. The traits and circumstances would include the strength of their respective egos—their capacity to tolerate anxiety as well as to repress, without which latter capacity (Segal, 1991, p. 31) symbolization is impossible (see chapter 6). Also relevant would be their lives prior to and following the traumas, including the presence or absence of emotional supports. Neither student was a creative writer, though the woman had the skill, even talent, to order her experience in an artful way and to gain some distance from it. The man presumably did not and so couldn't make use of language, at least, in the service of mastery. But these examples do illustrate how a creative act like writing can bring us up against resistance or help us to overcome it, be made easier by who we are and by our circumstances, even in the face of trauma, or be hindered by these.

For a week during my teaching career, I took over an absent colleague's creative writing class. One of the students with whom I held a conference during that week was a young man who handed in some poems which seemed promising but suffered both from too great a desire to imitate Emily Dickinson and too little a sense of what might constitute his own subject matter and voice. I asked him to tell me about himself. He seemed surprised but gave me enough information to suggest that his life and that of his poet role model could hardly have been less similar. When I asked him where in his work there was an inkling of the ghetto he'd grown up in, the war he'd served in, the streets or people he'd lived among, or of what it meant to be him, he looked incomprehending, then stunned. He told me it had never occurred to him that his own experiences might provide the subject matter for a poem. His own material or content, his inner life, perhaps as a black man in a society that devalued him and his experience, and certainly did not expect him, during that historical time at least, to make art of it, had not seemed to him interesting or worthy enough to be written about. Certainly nothing of his own experience seemed to him to be related to what he'd been exposed to thus far under the rubric of literature.

If this is a form of resistance to content, and I think that it is, it has undoubtedly helped to silence generations of writers and other artists whose life experiences and sensibilities have seemed to them, because of the prevailing literary, artistic, and social climates, as well as because of problems in self-esteem, not to be legitimate or worthwhile sources of art. To comment further, however, on how social forces and the forming of self-esteem interact in this context and contribute to creative blocks is beyond my scope here.

A related but somewhat different example, and the last I will mention from my college teaching career, concerns a young woman in a remedial writing class. The assignment was to keep a journal describing a two-week period in the student's life and to hand in some portion of it to be read, but not graded. The intent was to encourage students to write more freely, developing their awareness of sensory detail, their ability to describe. This student told me she'd been unable to do the assignment. Nothing, she reported, happened in her life. I asked her if she could describe what she had done after getting up that morning. She told me with a sigh which seemed to say, okay, I'll show you what I mean, that she had showered, dressed, baked cookies for her niece's birthday. She seemed astonished when

I asked if she could describe the shower, how the water felt, or the soap or shampoo, what any light might have been like, what thoughts she had had, what sensations, then what the kitchen was like, how the cookie ingredients had looked, felt, and smelled, then the dough.

I couldn't tell whether her astonishment was primarily at my asking, at her own tentative ability then to describe these things, or at the very idea that such a morning might contain something worth writing about. She told me her family never talked about things, not the events of their day nor their thoughts nor feelings. She believed she had nothing whatsoever to talk about. When I pointed out that she had just shown us both that this might not be the case, she looked intrigued, but also anxious. Like writers who describe their elation when they are first wanting to write and come across a poem describing something that is familiar to them—cutting vegetables, riding the bus (you mean, you can write about that?!)—my student had not until then considered that the content of her daily life might provide worthwhile material. Unlike such writers, however, my student probably did not turn this revelation into novels or poems. I can only hope that our exchange over her blank journal may have broadened her sense of what in and around her could prove worthy of attention.

Certainly the encounter suggested to me, her teacher, one of the things that makes many people feel they have nothing to say. Whatever internal conflicts she may have had, whatever inhibitions about her own thoughts, feelings, and ability to communicate—and these no doubt contributed—she was also someone who had experienced a kind of deprivation that made her feel contentless, not only in response to a class writing assignment, but perhaps also to any question that required her to focus inward.

While this example may seem unrelated to the question of what makes writing difficult for writers or painting for painters, it seems clear that when one's own perceptions, fantasies, wishes, and ideas *do not seem worth noting*—when one's self does not—then block or inhibition in the form of resistance to attending to or finding one's own content is a likely if not inevitable result.

Resistance to content, then, can take many forms, have many motivations and causes. A writer may resist recognizing and revealing certain feelings, ideas, wishes, ways of being, ways of thinking, because these are at odds with her sense of who she is or should be, how she needs to remember, to construe a relationship or an event. Content may be resisted because one imagines it will threaten, hurt, or destroy others, cause one to be abandoned, or otherwise endanger one's self. Content may be resisted because the artist fears that she may discover what she already suspects she knows but would rather not. Aspects of content and the relationships between these may stand for the inner world and the vitally important relationships represented there, relationships which may seem endangered by what the creative work reveals. Content may threaten to reveal specific aspects of the self, including some which may seem positive but are feared to be inimical to the sustaining of relationships with important others. Content may be resisted because it represents some dangerous wish or impulse, is associated with something painful which must be warded off, or perhaps because it stands for a part of the self which is feared to be empty. Wallace Stevens (1923/1990, p. 54) may have been suggesting this latter possibility (among many) in *The Snow Man*, when he describes, "the listener, who listens in the snow,/And, nothing himself, beholds/Nothing that is not there and the nothing that is." Thus, content may be resisted if we feel that it threatens to expose us to anxiety, guilt, abandonment, rejection, a sense of dangerous triumph or power, of isolation, merger, exposure, or shame; that is, any of the myriad things against which we may defend ourselves, in creative work as in the psychotherapeutic setting.

2

RESISTANCE AND THE UNCONSCIOUS MEANINGS OF THE WORK

> The resistance encodes the past that, by being repeated rather than remembered, is an obstacle to the future. (Phillips, 1993, p. 87)

Emotionally charged content isn't the only thing that mobilizes resistance to creative work. The creative process and product have complex unconscious meanings for each of us, meanings which contribute to the pleasure we find in doing the work and to our motivation for doing it, but contribute also to the anxiety that creative work involves. If the unconscious meanings to us of process or product are such that the work feels forbidden or dangerous, our anxiety will be intense and may lead to resistances, including the ones we call inhibition or block.

A painter, a promising advanced beginner, was feeling frustrated with her limited palette. She painted in pastels though she wanted to use more intense colors. Meanwhile, in her therapy, we were learning about her fears of strong feelings, of anger and hostility, sexual and competitive wishes, and excitement in the power of her intellect. To paint represented many things to this woman that she wasn't certain she was allowed. It meant to be more visible, forceful, successful, and out there, to be excited and alive, to surpass others. To paint boldly, as the more vibrant palette would permit her to do, threatened to expose her as no longer holding herself back in these ways, and the nature of her conflicts—she felt she had either to keep her desires and ambitions in check or she would become a tidal wave—made the prospect of the more intense colors feel dangerous.

She had first come for therapy because of depression, and though medication had been helpful, we found that each time she tried to take an important step forward, especially in her art, the medication would seem to fail her, and the depression would recur. It did now, thus checking her aspirations and punishing her for them. As we worked on the connections between her desire to move forward in her art, the meanings to her of doing so, and the depression, the latter began to lift and she started to paint, using the more vibrant palette she had been longing to try.

We worked then on her fear that she was greedy to want more in life than she already had, especially since she already had far more than was essential, and much that others lacked. Hers had been a family in which scarcity was a principle imposed in all areas. Children's individual needs, talents, or interests were disregarded, not because her parents lacked the money, but because deprivation was believed to build character. For her to deprive herself was painful but familiar. It was also gratifying. It made her imagine that she was being approved of, even preferred by, her parents.

As all this became clear, she began to want to explore other media in the visual arts, but worried that if she *could* work effectively in more than one, it would mean she was greedy indeed and must be punished, or punish herself for wanting more pleasure, and in this instance, more success than she felt she was allowed. She became depressed again, unable to paint or to venture into a new medium, thus once again keeping her seemingly dangerous wishes in check and punishing herself for having them. Her fear that wanting not only to paint well—she had recently begun to show her work and to win prizes—but to venture into another medium, would reveal her greed, was exacerbated by her actual greediness and considerable ambition, of which, at that time, she was only slightly aware. As we worked on all this, her depression lifted again. She became freer to explore other media, enjoyed doing so, and found that she was good at them, as earlier she had become freer to use, and successful at using, the more intense palette.

Subsequent steps in the therapy and in her development as an artist proceeded similarly. New material would emerge, revealing aspects of her psychology which were contributing to her unhappiness and to resistances to her art. These, we would find, had been preventing her from proceeding or even recognizing ways in which she wanted to proceed. As the new material emerged, or we began better to understand the old, she would initially feel depressed, and torment and sabotage herself until she could get nothing done in her studio. We would explore what it might mean to her to move forward. She would discover that her fears had to do not with the future, but with feelings and fantasies about the past. Then she would discover new interests and aspirations and successfully pursue these. Though for several years she made herself pay in this way for each advance, ultimately each helped free her of many constraints, as a person and an artist.

I saw another woman in therapy who seemed to have a talent for and interest in a number of creative areas, but could allow herself to pursue none of them. Her mother had been a successful performance artist who needed the stage, literally and figuratively, to herself. The daughter unconsciously believed that to do creative work of any sort was to compete with the mother, and that to do so, or even to seek attention in her mother's presence, was dangerous and forbidden. Even after her mother had long been dead, she felt that she was being aggressive and attempting the forbidden if she tried to do creative work. She felt this not only because her mother had seemed to need the limelight, but because of guilt about her own unconscious competitive wishes utterly to outdo her mother, and to punish the mother for having been unavailable during her childhood.

This woman was also struggling with unconscious angry and critical feelings which she feared might be exposed by creative work. Because such feelings were intolerable to her, she would project them onto others, especially teachers in the various media she tried briefly to study. If the teachers made even mild suggestions about her efforts, she experienced these as wrathfully, punishingly critical and scathing—her own painful, warded-off feelings toward them and others coming back to haunt her. She couldn't let herself know these feelings were her own. Instead, like many others who project their anger, then find even mild criticism intolerable, she would feel crushed by the criticism, and flee the class or workshop, never to return to it or to the particular art form she'd been studying there. Only when she was able to reclaim such projected feelings enough to be able to tolerate criticism, and had worked through her conflicts about creative work, was she able to choose a medium she wanted to work in and begin to work in it without significant anxiety or guilt.

A young premed student sought help with anxiety and unresolved grief about his mother who had become psychotic while he was an adolescent and never recovered. He hoped therapy might also free him again to write poetry and to paint; he'd done neither since his mother's illness. The responses of teachers and others to his work had suggested he might have considerable talent, but he could hardly think about creative work now without intense anxiety. Creativity was closely associated with his mother. She had been a sculptor who identified with the work and the suffering of the artist, Claudine Claudel. She had seemed, in fact, to be proprietary about suffering and to equate it with creativity to the point of insisting they were inextricably entwined.

Our work proceeded smoothly for a year, during which the young man's distress about his mother, and anxieties about relationships and applying to medical school, seemed understandably to take precedence over his conflicts about doing creative work. His grief was intense but rarely accessible. When he was aware of it, he found it helpful to be able to feel it and to cry in my presence. Anger, however, at his mother's having become psychotic during his late adolescence, and having in many ways been unavailable throughout his childhood, was initially beyond his awareness.

As we spoke of his anxieties, he began to realize that they had to do with strong feelings and impulses he was warding off. These included grief and finally anger at his mother, as well as sadness and anger about having had to be the good and undemanding child who stayed attuned to others at the expense of his own needs, including now the need to express himself creatively. He could occasionally see that complicating the picture were aggressive feelings toward his artist mother—problematical feelings for obvious reasons—as well as toward me, and that these contributed to his anxiety and possibly also to his holding himself back from his art.

In time he began, obliquely at first, and then directly, to express negative feelings about me and my work with him. These had come up before, but always mixed with humor, hope, or affection. Now he was fed up with who I was, how I spoke and worked, what I couldn't and wouldn't do for him. He disliked the kind of therapy I did. He was upset by similarities he perceived between me and an aunt who had stepped in during his mother's bouts of mental illness. He had resented this aunt for her presence and her attempts, which he found intrusive, to get him to talk about how he felt, and he resented me for expecting him to talk now.

In the sense I began to have of him at this time I was reminded of life with a young adolescent who is trying desperately to separate from and hold onto a parent with whom he is intensely involved. (Everything about me felt wrong to him, everything I said was absolutely the wrong thing to say to him; in fact he could barely stand to be in the room with me.) I began to feel blocked in relationship to him, to hesitate to speak, to fear that what I might express would be all wrong, that maybe *I* was all wrong. I began to wonder whether I had anything useful to say or to offer him.

These were feelings I knew from my own episodes of writer's block and I was certain they were also part of his. I was sure, too, that my feelings at this time, of being inadequate to the task I had taken on with him, the wrong person doing absolutely the wrong kind of work with him, were ones he must often have felt with his mother whom, throughout his childhood, he had tried desperately, but futilely, to protect.

He knew there was something extraordinary about his being able to carry on with me as he was doing, angrily and critically and almost unrelentingly, except for acknowledging occasional fear that he might be hurting me or that I would throw him out. It was extraordinary because he had never acted this way before. He had always been the loving, thoughtful son who charmed adults. An only child, he had spent his childhood and adolescence taking care of his mother, warding off the very same critical, angry, irritable feelings he had now in abundance toward me. To experience them with his fragile mother, the mother he had so wanted to save, would have been unthinkable. He spoke constantly of quitting therapy and finding someone else who would be better for him, someone who, unlike me, would help him feel understood and cared about, but he stayed.

On the rare occasions when he would give me a glimpse of his life apart from his anger at me, it seemed to be proceeding quite well with progress evident in a number of important areas. What he was perhaps most loathe to let me in on was that, despite the demands of school, he was writing, and doing so more excitedly, consistently, and successfully than ever before. He had also begun to paint again a little as well. He was relatively certain, however, that the considerable progress he knew he was making had little, if anything, to do with me or our work.

I came to believe that his resistance to writing and probably to painting, also, had partially involved a fear of exactly the storm of anger and criticism I was receiving. To be an artist, he sensed, required that he be honest with himself, and to do so meant facing the rageful, critical, and disappointed feelings of which I was now the recipient, as well as facing his longing and grief. That he could feel these emotions and survive them, that I could receive these and not be destroyed as he'd feared his fragile mother would have been, (in fact as he feared his mother *had* been) helped reassure him enough for him to be able to proceed.

To do creative work had unconsciously meant many problematical things for him. These had previously mobilized his resistance to such work, and could, of course, again. To do creative work meant to be vitally alive when his mother was not. It meant to have either to endure the kind of suffering the mother had insisted was the inevitable accompaniment, even the prerequisite, to creative work or to prove the mother wrong in this and himself the too fortunate one who could be creative and experience pleasure and excitement, not just suffering and grief.

To be creative had meant to be as one with his mother, which meant to suffer and be mad, but it also meant to become engrossed in something exciting which might potentially allow him for a time to forget her. This felt not only disloyal but also as if it might cost him one of the remaining links to her, which was unhappiness.

Creative work, therefore, unconsciously represented an act of aggression in many ways and an act of triumph and survival. These meanings did indeed make him anxious and had previously kept him mostly silent. I weathered his attacks week after week, without falling apart or throwing him out, however, and did not turn him into the caregiver in the relationship or absorb him into me as he felt his mother had tried to do. I continued to believe we had a relationship and were involved in important work together, but were separate. As a result, his fear of what had felt like unbearable feelings diminished enough for him to be able to explore them. He did this in part through his continued criticism of me and through our work together, but also through his writing and painting.

He described very movingly some of the things he had written, and even sent me some poems and a small painting during a summer when he was away visiting his father. Though he continued to doubt that I was helping him, he was aware that *something* important was happening, whether despite or because of the stormy hours we were spending together. In time, he decided to trust the evidence—the emerging of the creative self he'd longed for help in setting free—rather than his sense in the hours that I was all wrong for him, not helping him, and generally useless. I believed, though he was initially dismissive when I tried to tell him so, that he had perhaps needed to be able to separate from his mother in this way, by venting frustrated, hurt, angry feelings which he needed to see did not destroy me as an individual or our relationship, in order for his fear of his creative work and his resistance to it to diminish.

An academic came for therapy because, though engrossed in his work, he was dissatisfied with himself, his relationships, and his life. He told me months into the therapy that he'd once been involved in drawing and painting. As he talked about this, I sensed that his involvement had been passionate, that he'd had great aspirations for his art. He rarely let himself do it now; he missed making art, but when he tried, he'd begin to enjoy himself, then become frustrated by how far short of his aspirations the work fell, and then he'd give up in despair or disgust. He knew his expectations were unreasonable, considering how little attention he gave to his art. He knew, too, that high expectations, and unhappiness when he failed to meet them, were the reason he was in therapy.

This man had the usual complement of practical reasons why he could only rarely do what he loved, and these, though at times compelling, were also defensive. He was conflicted about doing his art and so, like many people, he let practical considerations stop him even when he might have arranged things differently. He wasn't only troubled by his own impossibly high standards, which in the course of the therapy became more realistic and attainable, making it easier for him to attempt work which he couldn't be sure would turn out to be perfect or great. He was conflicted about pleasure. Pleasure, which drawing and painting gave him, seemed to have been repudiated in his family. To experience it, as creative work caused him to do, meant to lose a sense of connection with his depressed, emotionally distant mother, as well as to seem to forgive her in ways he couldn't allow himself. These conflicts about his art never became central to the therapy because he had more pressing concerns. Also, his art was associated with feeling fully alive, which he feared, including within the relationship with me. We did, though, occasionally talk about why he so rarely allowed himself the pleasure his art afforded, and he began, gradually, to draw and paint a little more often and to enjoy doing so.

He came from a family where scarcity was a central theme. There was too little love, attention, or interest to go around. His parents, reportedly depressed, defeated people, had seemed not to know what to make of their artistic and intellectual son. Nor were his accomplishments recognized by his brothers, whom he had surpassed, both academically and financially.

For this man to allow himself the pleasure and excitement of more regularly doing his creative work and so developing his artistic potential, therefore represented further outdoing his parents and brothers. The extent to which he had already done so, though gratifying, made him feel guilty and even more estranged from them. He feared that if he allowed himself more pleasure and success, he would increase not only the emotional distance between himself and them, but also his own sense of aliveness, access to his imagination, and freedom. To do so would have threatened, in ways that clearly made him anxious, his view of himself as a sufferer from a family of sufferers.

His art had other problematic unconscious meanings for him. To allow himself to draw or to paint threatened his control over what, under a surface of reserve, were passionate, sensitive, and painfully vulnerable feelings, because art made him feel intensely emotional, and he feared this. He also feared his critical feelings. He projected these onto people around him, then worried that if he revealed, in his art, his own imperfections, those onto whom he projected would view him as harshly and contemptuously as he sometimes silently viewed himself and them. He may have imagined that it was his imperfections which made his mother depressed and caused his parents to relate to him in a distant, reserved, and seemingly rejecting way. If so, to expose these imperfections, as artists inevitably feel they do in their work, was to risk further hurt and disappointment in the world. Finally, to allow himself the pleasure and excitement he experienced in doing art may have unconsciously meant relinquishing a last chance to reproach and punish others with his unhappiness, and elicit their care.

In my own experience, years of what I considered to be writer's block, though I wasn't attempting to write, ended when analysis helped me to discover that writing felt dangerous to me in part because it represented, and required, leaving people out. Writing represented being more attuned to my own internal life than to theirs, something which we who become therapists, or we who, early in life, needed to be attentive to or worried about another, may find problematical. To be immersed in my writing requires that for hours at a time, I forget about being therapist, wife, mother, friend, teacher, forget my role as properly acculturated female, closely reading the needs of other people, forget about protecting them from what I may discover I really think or feel. This is part of what, for years, kept me from writing, and it is also part of what makes writing exciting to me: Writing is a glorious opportunity to leave others out and to live alone in my poem. But the excitement of this had to outweigh the anxiety and to become acceptable to me before I could allow myself to have it. I had to feel that excluding others for hours from my attention or awareness would not necessarily reveal to them my essential disloyalty in preferring my own company to theirs, my thoughts to theirs, my pleasure in writing to their pleasure, real or imagined, in having me always available to them. I had to feel that tuning others out would not necessarily hurt or destroy them, leaving me alone in the universe. Of course, while fears that excluding others is aggressive and will hurt or alienate them can result from our knowledge of their vulnerability, such fears can also result from our own aggression or competitiveness. Then we may feel the need to protect others or to remain close and attentive in order to make amends.

I started writing again, and then a variation on this concern with excluding others presented itself. I began to imagine that if I let myself take my writing seriously, I'd be forgotten by my professional community. I'd never get another referral from a colleague or be asked to teach or to supervise again. I felt I would disappear from the awareness of others through spending my time writing rather than attending seminars and conferences, through choosing to do an M.F.A. in poetry rather than joining my friends and colleagues in pursuing psychoanalytic training—the obvious next step for one in my field who is seriously committed to the work. As I thought about this, I began to realize that the underlying worries were actually quite different. I was afraid *I* would forget *them*. I'd become so engrossed in writing that colleagues, friends, and patients would disappear from my awareness, as indeed they do while I actually write. Their anticipated forgetting of me was the retaliation I felt my forgetfulness must deserve.

The sense of danger many feel when we do, or want to do, creative work, often derives from our own fantasies and wishes about excluding others, competing with and outdoing them, winning their love, displacing them, being so close to them that we fear we will destroy them or so separate that we fear we already have. Where creative work unconsciously represents such things to us, we may be unable to do it, do it with considerable difficulty, or do it at great cost. Sometimes the situation is even more complex: The unconscious belief that creative work is dangerous, comes not only from our own fantasies and wishes. Sometimes it comes, at least in part, from actual experiences with the environment, and what we do with these in our imagination. Certain experiences can make withdrawal into creative work and the pleasure and excitement in doing such work seem dangerous indeed.

During my clinical training, I observed a series of mother–toddler play groups which were offered one morning a week for 10 weeks as a service to local families. My task was, unobtrusively, if possible, to make observations for use in developing a set of rating scales. The toddlers, who were 16 to 24 months of age, played in a comfortable room with toys, while half the mothers stayed with them and the other half met in an adjoining room and talked informally with a child development specialist. After 30 minutes, everyone gathered in the playroom for a snack; then the two groups of mothers switched places.

One pair concerned me from the start. The toddler, a boy, was 16 months old when the group first met. Of the 10 pairs I observed in the group, this boy and his mother were the only ones who consistently arrived with the child in his mother's arms, where, though he was able to walk, he mostly stayed. This mother and son were often dressed in clothes made from matching fabric, as if the two had been cut from the same cloth. The mother was a single parent who seemed to cling to her child because of her own need rather than because of any apparent need of his. When snack time came and the other children and mothers gathered together, this one mother would take her son aside and feed him separately, though she didn't seem to feed him anything that suggested a special diet. Often in fact she removed him to a corner to give him basically the same sort of snack the others were enjoying together in a friendly and sometimes exuberant group.

Whenever this little boy would pay attention to anything other than his mother—the other toddlers playing nearby with the toys, the toys themselves, the other mothers—he did so in a way that

seemed surreptitious: quickly, and with hasty, covert glances at his
mother as if in fear that she might notice. And she did inevitably
notice, and react dramatically. The moment his attention was engaged elsewhere, even in this tentative and seemingly worried way,
his mother's demeanor would change. She would slump, twist, almost recoil away from him, and look angry or depressed. In an
instant, he'd look back in her direction in alarm, as if he sensed the
change, and since he was rarely more than a few inches away from
her, he probably did feel her stiffen or move away. He would then
stroke or pat her, as if to reassure her, or he'd cling to her, turning
from the temptation to explore the varied and colorful outside
world. At this, she would gather him up, fuss over him, and seem
happy again, though she sometimes seemed to make a show of sigh-
ing, as if in resignation, when he would cling to her. Twice I saw her
persist in looking away, as if angrier or more hurt than usual, and I
watched him pull her face back toward him and stroke it, as if to
coax her back into engaging with him. He didn't do this playfully,
as other toddlers sometimes did; there was an urgency about his
behavior at these moments. It was only with the persistent encouragement of the leader and other mothers that this mother was ever in
the discussion group without her child in her lap. When she occasionally was in the group she seemed hopelessly distracted and kept
making what seemed to me to be visual appeals to her child through
the doorway, until he would burst from the mother who had been
chosen to try and engage him, and rush to his own.

Such interactions occurred consistently over the 10 weeks. Not
once did I see this child play with a single toy, interact with another
toddler, even in the in passing, quasi-collision way of children of this
age, not even with his mother at his side. Not once did his mother
initiate or otherwise show interest in contact with another adult,
though several tried to engage her. Nor did the mother indicate,
though tactfully given openings to do so, that there might be some
unusual difficulty at present. And once, when the group leader asked
her how her week had been, I heard this mother express bewilderment about her son's apparent interest in a friend, a man who had
visited them, asking why her son would want to play with the male
friend when he had her.

I know nothing further about *this* family, but I've worked in
therapy with adults who were made to feel in their early relationships
the way this toddler must have felt, and who, as a result, found it
excruciatingly difficult to exist as separate people with their own
thoughts, because to do so seemed to threaten them with abandonment. On the basis of such clinical experiences and of developmental
theory, I can speculate about what might have happened to this
toddler if the interactions I observed were, and continued to be

typical. I can speculate with confidence, too, about the implications of such experience for creative work.

Later, if something caught his attention—his own thoughts, an image or impression or color, another person—he would be likely to grow anxious and unable to stay with whatever had so engaged him. He would be unlikely, that is, to feel free to attend to his inner experience or to the outer world because he would be too busy trying, even in her absence, to attend to his mother for fear otherwise of harming or losing her. Anxiety would be intense and interfere with his ability to learn, to develop relationships, except perhaps extremely entangled ones, and certainly to do imaginative work. He would be stopped from doing such work *both* by an accurate sense that his immersion in it threatened, or had threatened, a vital relationship, and by difficulty with his own fantasies about his aggression, the damage to others inherent in his enjoying himself elsewhere. True, whether he would respond in this way would depend in part on his innate temperament and subsequent experience, but he would be likely, I believe, to be encumbered by the problems I have described.

Creative work means sometimes leaving others out. If important others are experienced or imagined as not being able to survive this, if a relationship is felt not able to survive, how is one to be alone, concentrate on one's imaginative life—indeed even have such a life—and get absorbed in one's own creativity? How is one to be able to experience that "transitional space" between inside and outside, self and other, subjective and objective, in which space play becomes possible and creativity occurs (Winnicott, 1971a), if the other won't stay put when we try? How are we to do creative work if the unconscious meanings of becoming engaged in doing something include being abandoned by the other or damaging the other by our inattention, or, as it sometimes seems, our aggression? If such meanings are attached to creative or any engrossing work, then that work is apt unconsciously to represent to us the destruction of vital relationships, subsequent isolation, or even a kind of annihilation, and so become impossible, or at least our capacity to do it will be significantly impaired.

A less extreme example than that of the toddler in the play group is that of an 8-year-old brought by her parents for therapy because she seemed irritable, unhappy, and "uncommunicative" at home, though she was doing well at school and showed no other signs of difficulty. Her father had been very close to his mother as a boy, or rather he'd felt that he was, but their closeness required that he tell her *everything.* For him to claim any right to privacy apparently felt to her like a rejection and she would withdraw in response, though not as pathologically as the mother of the toddler mentioned above.

This man knew only one model for closeness between parent and child, and that was the one he had learned with his own mother. He asked his daughter endless questions about how she felt and what she thought. She answered grudgingly. If she didn't answer, he worried that unless he persisted, she'd think he didn't care, and so persist he did. I didn't have the impression that his intention was to violate his daughter's privacy; he felt rather that he was showing interest in her and that to do otherwise was to be neglectful. Of course, he wasn't my patient, and I don't know what unconscious meanings the intrusiveness that he had experienced and was perpetuating may have had for him.

In time I was able to ask him how he'd felt about his mother's insistance on such "sharing" and he told me he'd disliked it. I told him that I didn't think his daughter liked it either and that rather than feel cared about when he did this, I thought she felt intruded upon until it was almost unsafe to have thoughts or feelings. When I felt I had enough rapport with him, I was able, with his wife's help, to advise him to back off, and he was apparently able, with occasional lapses and some relief, to do so.

Toward the end of the therapy, I gave the girl a gift, a diary with a lock and key. I told her it was a private place where she could write whatever she wanted. She asked if she was supposed to show it to me or to tell me or her father what she wrote there. I said no, she could tell me things if and when she wanted to, and her father as well, but the diary was private and hers alone. Her expression as she left my office with locked diary in one hand and key in the other hand was luminous.

If this girl grew up to have an interest in creative pursuits, I'd like to imagine that our work together and my intervention with her father helped to make them possible for her. However, she may instead have come to feel that absorption in such work or even having her own opinions and ideas threatens her with the withdrawal or anger of others. She may have come to fear that in doing such work she hurts others who she imagines need to be, and perhaps even have the right to be, privy to her inner life.

A colleague spoke to me after I presented the paper from which this book evolved. She told me of her own writer's block, which she thought was connected with her mother's having, when shown my colleague's writing over the years, responded not to what was stated, but rather to what the mother divined—and often divined correctly—had been left unsaid. The writer was understandably shaken by the intrusiveness of this, the violation of her own silence, but rather than choosing not to show her mother what she wrote, she stopped writing. To write and not show what she had written apparently represented an exclusion that felt intolerable in its seeming aggressiveness. Not writing may also have been a way of punishing the mother, though if so, it was clearly punishing the daughter more, because it saddened her greatly to achieve her privacy at such a cost.

The belief that creative work represents the damaging exclusion of others and is therefore dangerous and proscribed needn't originate in intrusiveness or in punitive or depressed withdrawal on the part of parents. Even well-meaning parents may inadvertently suggest that their child's privacy hurts or threatens them, that separateness endangers, that connection requires that all be shared. They may convey the message that they will be less interested in a child who keeps certain things to herself, or overly interested in one who tells all and offers up her innermost self. Such behavior can further complicate the already complex matter of their child's conflicting needs for separateness and closeness, autonomy and dependency, and fears of abandonment and merger.

I was told of a mother who thought that everything her daughter wrote was about her, even when it clearly was not, suggesting both the mother's need to be included and a reluctance or inability on her part to consider her daughter as having concerns or interests which were either separate or solitary. Such complications make creative work difficult because the work may then take on conflictual unconscious meanings, such as that one is being intolerably aggressive in doing it, is driving others away by being engrossed in work that excludes them, or risks being forgotten by not remaining continually available and engaged.

Depression or withdrawal by a parent, especially in early childhood, can be experienced similarly and make it difficult for the child not to attend to or worry about the parent. As a result, involvement elsewhere, including in creative work, may feel like an abandonment for which we will be abandoned in turn. Difficulties occur at the opposite pole, too, with parents or important others who show no interest in a child's imagination or in expressions of a child's inner life, or who are dismissive or contemptuous of a child's attempts to give that life voice. Such unhelpful influences may be more readily apparent, however, than those I've been considering.

Anxiety about and problems in doing creative work may result from the unconscious meanings such work or the products of it have for us. Our ideas about creative work can cause us to experience the pleasure or excitement the work affords us as dangerous. We may worry about what it means to feel big or powerful, sexy or threatening. Creative work may represent to us the offering of a gift or bribe. It may symbolize to us a seduction, a placation, an attempt to hurt others. Creative work may unconsciously be considered a way of getting the attention of one parent away from the other—the longed-for and dreaded oedipal victory—or from a brother or sister. If this is considered unacceptable or dangerous, the work may be sacrificed or held in check, the early promise not realized, the successful book followed by painful, self-punishing silence. Such manifestations of resistance to the meanings of creative work are myriad. When we consider them in all their array, it may seem remarkable that anyone manages to do creative work at all.

3

THE PAGE OR CANVAS AS MIRROR: REVISION AND CHARACTER

Sometimes what we're up against when we do creative work is not fear of certain content or dread of whatever the creative act means to us. Sometimes, and perhaps especially when we revise, we're up against who we are, how we are organized as people—what psychoanalysis calls "character" or "defense style." Former U.S. Poet Laureate Robert Hass once told a workshop that he often sits down to his latest draft of a poem and says, "Oh, no, me again." We meet ourselves on the page, and we meet our limitations, our character, as well.

I was in a workshop once with the poet Frank Bidart. He said of a poem of mine, which ventured into personally difficult territory, that my use of connectives there was serving to vitiate feeling. I said, surprising myself, but apparently not him, "You're asking me to change the way I live my life." And he said, "Yes." Those of us who feel we will self-immolate if our strong feelings aren't kept in check may indeed overuse connectives. We may, when we try to deal with this in revising, find the connectives hard to relinquish. They serve a purpose. The problem may be that the purpose they serve is inimical to the poem, as the use of defensive strategies or mannerisms could be, say, to the way a therapist talks to or writes about patients. I did take the connectives out; I sat with intense feelings of anxiety, then discovered that the poem was better, that using fewer connectives, even allowing intense feelings to exist unchecked, didn't kill me, or my mother. I think it was Louise Glück who said at that same conference that we can change who we are through revision just as we can change our poems by changing who we are. Yeats (1940/ 1979, untitled poem) said it, too:

> The friends who have it I do wrong
> Whenever I remake a song,

27

Should know what issue is at stake;
It is myself that I remake.[1]

A poet wrote chronically obscure poems. She seemed to be trying to achieve mystery, that quality which can so deepen art, but the
poems didn't invite the reader, as mystery does, to ponder various
possibilities; they excluded instead and so failed to communicate.
This quality in the work was slightly maddening. These were promising poems, inviting at first, sometimes beautiful, but the obscurity
defeated them and no amount of workshop feedback to this effect
made the least difference. I came to believe, as I learned a little
about her life, that the obscurity was something over which this poet
had no control and which served a defensive purpose, in quite a
pervasive way. She had been molested as a child. She'd come from
a family where the revealing of this had gotten her banished. She
couldn't tell what happened to her in her life without results that
were overwhelming; and she couldn't let her poems tell either. The
poems were busy *trying* to obscure, and they succeeded at this, to
their detriment as art.

A prose writer's father had been very seductive. When she was
16, he liked to climb into her bed with her to chat. He wouldn't
touch her, he'd just lie beside her, talking. Long before I heard
about this, I wondered why, in her otherwise wonderful stories, there
always seemed to be some essential information left out, something
the reader, or at least I as reader, needed to know in order to understand what was going on. I'd try to tell her what I felt was missing
or needed to be done and she'd get upset. In time, I believe that
her therapy helped her to realize that this problem in her work had
to do with things in her life she didn't want to know or say.

This reticence or inability manifested itself differently with her
than with the poet who'd been molested. That woman wrote poems
which left the reader at an almost complete loss as to what was going
on. This prose writer allowed you to follow clearly and closely, then
suddenly there would be a leap of some sort in the narrative, and
you'd be confused as to how the protagonist got from there to here.
(I am *not* suggesting that a tendency to write in these ways means
there's a sexual secret in the writer's past. I am suggesting that where
such attributes persist in the writing, despite the writer's efforts to
change them, there are likely to be psychological reasons which may
need to be understood and worked on if the writing is to change.)

---

[1]Reprinted with permission of Simon & Schuster from *The Variorum Edition of
the Poems of W. B. Yeats,* edited by Peter K. Alt and Russell K. Alspach. Copyright 1940
by Georgie Yeats; copyright renewed © 1968 by Bertha Georgie Yeats, Michael Butler
Yeats, and Anne Yeats.

A woman in an ongoing workshop had written a promising poem about her glamorous, sexy, popular older sister. You could tell the poem wanted to confess that the poet had hated this sister as much as loved her, envied her as much as admired her, wanted her dead as much as wanted to praise her. But the poem was being denied this dimension, this emotional richness, because the poet was someone who, characteristically as far as I could tell from all her poems and comments, needed not to confess to the negative sides of herself. She was trying desperately to be nice, and the poem suffered for it, as I suspect the poet did, too.

Another poet in a workshop wrote poems which were arresting but had seemingly impenetrable surfaces. The images he focused on in his work were sophisticated, even gorgeous, but the feelings, psychological states, dramatic situations, or spiritual conditions they intended to represent seemed inaccessible. Nor did closer reading yield access, though something seemed to be hinted at which made readers willing to try to get past whatever was keeping them at bay. When this difficulty was pointed out to the poet in the workshop—that the surfaces invited and intrigued but not enough was given to allow the reader access to whatever lay beneath—he seemed interested and thanked the workshop for this observation.

Afterwards, he told me that the objections were familiar, yet he couldn't quite understand them. He asked if I'd understood and agreed with the criticism which had been offered. I said I thought I had, and did. He asked if I'd be willing to explain it to him; I agreed to try.

This was a man with whom I'd had good conversations about the workshop and poetry. Yet the conversations, which seemed perhaps to initiate a friendship, ultimately did not lead to any furthering of a connection. He would express an interest in staying in touch but not follow through. So in my personal dealings with him, I was having an experience which seemed consistent with the observation made in the workshop about his poems—something was presented which invited further looking or knowing. Then he seemed to retreat; the offer would be silently withdrawn. When we spoke, I explained the criticism as I'd understood it. I told him that the surfaces he described were inviting, even intriguing, that they suggested depths into which one wished to be invited but clearly was not. The poems seemed not to yield even to patient, interested, close scrutiny. He sighed, agreed, and told me this was exactly what he was working on in psychoanalysis. The poems couldn't allow closeness, knowledge, or intimacy and the poet couldn't either, though both poet and poems seemed to invite one to want to know them better. I know nothing about this man's history, but was not surprised that my personal experience with him paralleled the workshop criticism and the state and focus of his psychoanalysis. His attempts at revision hadn't yet been able to carry him past this characteristic resistance to going deeper into himself, his art, or his relationships with people. He could present that which intrigued and attracted, but could show only its surface; the depths were sealed off. This problem didn't stop him from writing, though it did stop him from writing as effectively as he wished.

I was in a workshop with a woman who wrote excellent first drafts, was able to revise these effectively using workshop feedback, but would inevitably need additional feedback in order to go further. She could do what the group suggested or solve problems the group pointed out, but then seemed unable further to discover what the poem might need or to carry what she had learned into the next poem without more help. If she did occasionally make progress on her own, she would need reassurance that what she had done was effective. She wouldn't or couldn't try on her own to work the poems farther along, though she could effectively use suggestions from others, however slight, to make significant progress. She showed less ambition for her poems beyond revising them according to workshop feedback than the poems clearly deserved. It was as if she needed our permission to think, to proceed with her work at each step.

In her interpersonal dealings during workshop coffee breaks, a similar quality was apparent: She'd look to others for direction, support, and advice in a nonreciprocal manner, as if she were perpetually a dependent younger sister or mentee in need of guidance and attention. She would linger at the end of a session as if to extract any residual help and advice from others before they slipped out of reach. When the workshop disbanded, this talented poet feared she wouldn't write anymore because she wasn't certain she could do so on her own. I don't know enough about her life to speculate with confidence on the meanings or origins of her difficulty. It was clear, though, that the same aspect of her character, or neurosis, which was noteworthy in her dealings with people in the workshop, hindered her proceeding as a poet beyond the stage of apprentice or student.

A man I saw in therapy wrote very brief poems which were clever and witty, but limited. They seemed not to want to dwell in any one place or on any one observation for long, and disinclined to go too deeply into anything. This man told me emphatically that he *never* revised. He feared that to do so would ruin the poems, spoiling his fresh first impression or sense of things. In therapy, he frequently alluded to the sad circumstance under which his mother had married his father. She had, he said, been pregnant with him, the eldest of three, and so had been trapped into a union he was sure she must always have regretted. He felt sorry for her, guilty about having been the innocent cause of the marriage which he was convinced was an unhappy one, though there was nothing overt to suggest that this was the case. He was surprised she could have gotten into this sad situation since he was sure she had never been attracted to his father sexually, or presumably to any man. He imagined that her having gotten pregnant by the father represented some weirdly aberrant moment in their lives, certainly not one he cared to think about. His painful feelings about his mother's presumed unhappiness were part of a constellation of beliefs and fears which kept him out of romantic or sexual relationships. He was single, celibate, and lonely.

At some point, something, an irresistible impulse I suppose, prompted me to ask him when his parents had married and when he, the patient, had been born. He mentioned the date of each event, but without noticing that the marriage had taken place three years before his birth. Then something, perhaps my startled expression, perhaps a readiness to face this, made him stop and think about what he had just said. He looked stunned. His conviction that his parents had married because his mother was pregnant with him and would never have done so otherwise, had been a fantasy. To maintain the fantasy he had needed not to notice or think about certain obvious things, like the three-year interval between the marriage and his birth. To maintain the fantasy had required that he stick with his "first take" and never reconsider or revise. Though he had enjoyed modest success as a poet, this defensive need never to take a second look had limited what he could accomplish in his poems as it limited what he could enjoy elsewhere in his life.

A poet in a workshop was told, "You say it, then you seem not to trust you're being heard, so you say it again. Then you still aren't convinced, so you say it a third time. Trust your reader. Trust your poem." She told me that one of her central experiences growing up had been to feel she was not heard. Her hearing impaired father would sometimes make a show of turning off his hearing aid when he didn't like or wasn't interested in what his children were saying to him. Neither parent had tended to listen; both would interrupt, change the subject, or start doing something else while others spoke. This poet had rarely felt able to get a sentence in with her large family, before being cut off. She had developed a tentative way of speaking which may have pulled for this sort of experience as well as being a result of it.

In part as a consequence of such experiences, she was aware of having difficulty in believing she would be found interesting enough to hold the attention of listener or reader. She recognized that her poems were tentative and tended to repeat themselves, as if they, too, doubted that anyone was listening. She knew that this reduced her effectiveness and authority as a poet. She found it difficult to revise the poems so that they didn't seem to ask, "Is anyone listening? Is anyone interested in what I have to say?" but also found it exhilarating to try. Though this was a problem with which she continued to struggle, she found that focusing on it in revising gave her increased confidence. It also helped the poems sound more authoritative and stop apologizing for and repeating themselves. The workshop leader had apparently given her the equivalent of a good therapeutic interpretation which she had been able to use. The revising she did subsequently was like the working through that must go on in therapy before an insight can bring about change.

A somewhat different example concerns a woman whose inability to revise resulted less from her character traits or defensive style than from fundamental problems of early deprivation and self-esteem. After experimenting with many art forms, and showing talent for all but stamina for none, this woman had begun writing fiction. She worked excitedly on a first draft of a novel, producing hundreds of unrevised pages while enjoying fantasies of book parties, promotional talk shows, film options. She then found someone knowledgeable about publishing to read her unrevised first draft. She practically held her breath awaiting that person's judgment. He told her that her manuscript was promising, but needed work and lacked structure. Her mood plummeted. In this, she was like many writers at a first criticism, but then, rather than setting to work on revisions, she despaired and became disillusioned about that particular project, put it aside, and began a second novel. Later, under similar circumstances, she would begin a third. Each followed the same course; she couldn't bear to revise; needing to do so somehow represented defeat or failure, the often referred to "narcissistic injury." If the first draft weren't perfect and applauded, she couldn't bear to stay with and work on it; she had instead to go on to something new.

She would send first drafts of short fiction to magazine editors and upon receiving one rejection notice would be devastated and retire the piece. Writer friends told her of their numerous drafts, their stacks of rejection notices before any success, but she couldn't apply this principle to herself. The work had to be perfect in its original form, otherwise, she lost all interest in it.

It seemed she had difficulty tolerating frustration in any form. She'd dropped out of college rather than take the two remaining courses required for a degree because she didn't care for their subject matter. This was partially out of a need to defeat herself, to undermine her goals. It also had to do with a general inability to tolerate frustration. When frustrated, she needed quickly to reassure herself that there was gratification (and love) available in some other form, hence the tendency to start a new manuscript, as earlier she had tended to start working in a new medium when frustrated with the old. Her mood about her work seemed to shift rapidly from an idealized sense of what she had made, with fantasies that it would bring her love, fame, and fortune, to a sense of disappointment and despair when the work wasn't taken by book editors upon first query and in first draft.

I learned that she'd had a troubling childhood. Her father, a charming philanderer, had deserted the family when she was quite young. He had been an idealized man who had abruptly fallen from grace in his daughter's eyes. My impression was that she hadn't had the opportunity in childhood we all need, to be disillusioned gradually and in tolerable doses. It's a process that optimally allows us to accept the limitations of things and people we have put our hopes in, to retain faith in them and in ourselves, even when we encounter imperfection or disappointment. Perhaps the rejections by readers and editors felt like the terrible one she had suffered at the hands of her father; this might help to account for her sense that what was rejected had no second chance ever of being chosen, although something did enable her to begin anew with the next piece of work. Yet because she couldn't revise that one either, the disappointment and rejection were likely to be perpetual. It seemed she felt that neither her fiction nor her childhood self could, once rejected, ever make itself good enough to be valued and accepted.

A man who was a remarkably lucid, intelligent thinker and astute about others, wrote poems in which his dramatic situations were clear but certain of his images were not. One squinted mentally to see what it was he had described, but the images remained out of focus. As I got to know him, I came to suspect that there were things this man needed not "to see" about himself. There was something exploitative in his treatment of others. Perhaps the blurry images, the unclear way he looked at things or let others look, were related to this. Revision did not seem greatly to improve the difficulty, despite this poet's intelligence, sensitivity, and verbal skill. He seemed, in this one way at least, to be stuck, and stuck as I have been describing in each of these examples: His attempts to revise brought him up against what was problematical in himself.

This takes different forms for each writer, as perhaps it does for each person involved in other kinds of creative work. Among poets, familiar examples include the following: We reread our work and see that we have, yet again, buried our endings. We have, as usual, clarified too much. We've told too much. We are still writing about our father and the poems are beginning to sound alike. We keep writing about different things, but the poems sound alike. Nobody can tell, though we think it should be quite clear, what is going on in the poems. They can tell quite well, as always, but seem dissatisfied;

they think we haven't risked enough and we haven't. We've revised our way, as we tend to do, from risk into safety.

As professionals or others trying to write papers, we may characteristically find it too hard to get started, decide our ideas are too obvious to matter, or too wonderful for words, or become discouraged when we find ourselves bogging down in details and never getting to the big picture. We may overexplain, be vague or too tentative. We may retreat if our first draft seems too pedestrian. We may be reticent to reveal ourselves, fear losing control over our material, or get off to a promising start and suddenly realize there simply isn't enough time.

It's in these often painful and maddening repetitions of who we are or where we are stuck that we find the fingerprints of our character or characteristic defenses, no less than we may find here the origins of individual style, the source of our best themes. Our wishes, fears, our defense styles leave traces in our work the way subatomic particles apparently do, allowing physicists to infer and even to prove their existence though they're never actually seen. Of course, this is so not only with creative writers or with other artists, but with how therapists speak to or write about patients, professors talk to students or write for colleagues, or parents interact with their children. We may be limited when we attempt to revise, as when we try to change our behavior, by a characteristic need to remain ambiguous, deny, avoid, obfuscate, distance ourselves from feelings or from ideas, to impress, placate, or control others, to elude ourselves and others, cover our bases, not commit ourselves, remain abstract. Any such trait in our character, if rigid, will likely manifest itself in limiting or distorting ways, which is, after all, the nature of rigidity. The process of revision may allow us to greatly change our work, to deepen it, discover through it what it is about, increase its clarity, mystery, beauty, or power. But where we find we cannot revise, or revise effectively, we may be up against more than the limitations of talent or technique; we may be up against what the mirror shows us, and the page.

Shapiro (1965) defines a person's style as "a form or mode of functioning—the way or manner of a given area of behavior—that is identifiable, in an individual, through a range of his specific acts . . .''; and "neurotic styles" as "those modes of functioning that seem characteristic, respectively, of the various neurotic conditions" (p. 1). So whether we are discussing neurosis or not, style is part of what is characteristic of the individual and will show up in creative work, in its strengths and weaknesses, as well as in other endeavors.

Since most of us tend to have at least some neurotic features, and since these are often what get in the way of creative work, my

point about resistance, revision, and character might be further elucidated by a consideration of some of the styles Shapiro has described. We can imagine, for example, what notes a hypothetical
writing teacher might make in the margins of work by a writer with
an "obsessional style," and what difficulty such a writer might have
responding to them when attempting to revise: "You are giving too
much detail to hold a reader's interest. Can you select what is salient
and omit the rest?" "This seems very factual, cerebral; it could use
some emotional coloring, something to make the reader feel what
you are trying to describe." "It's rather difficult here to see the
forest for the trees." "Your use of language here seems not lively
enough." "Is it possible to be less linear (orderly, controlled, cerebral, intellectualized)?" "This would be more effective if, instead of
always offering the reader alternatives, you stated what the weather
was like; you are, after all, the writer and have the power to choose."
"You may be exerting too much control here over your writing; ease
up, let the process take over, see what happens." "You keep
doubting and qualifying here in a way that undercuts the writing.
Could you see what happens if you take out the qualifiers and stop
second guessing yourself? The passage would be more effective."
"This could use some sense of mystery; we don't need to be told
every detail; leave something to the imagination." Or, "The reader
gets it the first time; this repeating undercuts your point and diminishes your authority."

A writer with a more "hysterical style" might encounter marginal notes like these: "Could you be more specific here?" "What
exactly do you mean when you say it was 'grand,' 'marvelous,' 'agonizing,' 'brilliant'? Show, don't tell." "Perhaps this is a little dramatic for the content; might you save the dramatic for more
significant moments so it is more persuasive?" "You reach these
rather general and sweeping conclusions. Might you give us something to show how you got there?" "This is very colorful and lively
but it might be more effective if you gave us some specific details."
"There seems to be an intriguing tension here but I need some
sense of what is generating it, what might be going on."

This doesn't cover all the possible styles which Shapiro considers
or which exist, or the various combinations of these, but it may
suggest how the organization of one's character and characteristic
ways of experiencing the world will color or decolor one's creative
work and present a challenge when one sits down to revise. The
writer who characteristically fears to reveal herself; who is too fearful
of making a fool of herself to risk letting important parts of her way
of being in the world be seen; who needs to qualify and qualify
because of a fear of being accountable or blamed, will be so in the
way she writes. She will encounter these elements in herself when

she attempts to revise. So will the writer who can't tolerate ambiguity, or is unable to be exact, clear, precise, or focused, or has to be far too much so, who has to see all that is negative as originating outside of herself, who needs to be in careful control of her thoughts and what comes out of her. It's not surprising, then, that the challenge which revision presents is one that can in many instances defeat the writer, who may give up or continue to produce work that suffers from the same characteristic traits, regardless of efforts to change, move ahead, or go deeper. In other media than writing, this will manifest itself differently, but it will manifest itself nonetheless.

Ehrenzweig (1967, pp. 24, 43, 56) has suggested that rigid characters tend quickly to perceive a familiar gestalt or to find premature closure in their perceptions of things, in order to render what they see as known, safe, and familiar. Such a need too often precludes their seeing things in new ways and so prevents their doing innovative work in the arts or anywhere that involves creativity. Flexibility, in contrast, can permit such character traits as I've described to be put to good use. The challenge of revision may then be to push or permit us to change both our writing and ourselves. Writing which is obsessive in quality may be excellent writing, as may writing that is strongly emotional and sweeping. Individual traits, including a penchant for detail or for strong feeling, a need for control or a capacity for release of control can, in creative work, be sources of strength and contribute to a distinctive style or voice. In relationship to creativity, as in relationship to other endeavors, whether such traits are assets or liabilities depends on whether they are rigid or flexible, whether we, the possessors of such traits, are the proverbial tail or the proverbial dog.

I tried a writing exercise once, to do several pages of "free writing," and to do them writing past the printed margins of the page. I found that doing this simple exercise made me initially anxious, then exhilarated. Neither of these responses on my part surprised me much, though their intensity did; I had by then been writing long enough to have a sense of how risk and experimentation, which this exercise in its small way represented, tend to affect me. The anxious part was the one which needs precise boundaries, is more at ease with what is familiar, conventional, and initially balks at departures or change of any kind. It can dread airports and goodbyes, hesitate in response to imposed changes in schedule or plan. The part that became exhilarated was the one, equally familiar, which delights in being what the French call a "flaneur," a wanderer without destination, the one who thrills at departure gates when the destination is foreign and far, enjoys new foods, sundry unexpected encounters. The simple exercise of writing past the margins brought me up against both a very familiar personal form of resistance which

I need to overcome whenever I depart from routine and each time I sit down to write, and an equally familiar source of pleasure and excitement, and on a good day, of poems. The exercise confronted me, as writing does, with myself—the parts that support and nurture my creative efforts and the ones that work tenaciously to undermine it. It brought me up against the ways I limit myself, the ways I am limited. It showed me the ways I am most open, flexible, and alive. It brought me to one of the borders between success and failure in my writing life, reminding me of what makes the process difficult, yet makes me, with countless others, persist at it, despite the anxiety it evokes.

4

THE ENVELOPING FOG: RESISTANCE AND REGRESSION

Surrender, not control.
(B. Hillman, 1988, personal communication)

Creative work brings us up against conflictual material, forces us to tolerate ambiguity, has potentially difficult and often unconscious meanings for us, and makes us see ourselves. Such work seems also to require that we give ourselves up at times to that inevitable and usually transient stepping or sliding back to earlier mental states or developmental stages that we call regression. It is regression and the feelings regression evokes that many who want to do creative work find frightening, and so avoid.

Regression can include feeling helpless and taken over, entering altered states in which we have weird thoughts like the ones we have in dreams where the rules of time and logic don't apply. Regression may involve feeling like a sudden conduit or medium for something else. The writer, when inspired, may momentarily feel, for example, like the Pythia, that priestess at Delphi who sat on her tripod stool inhaling the intoxicating fumes which arose from a crevice in the earth and, intoxicated, made strange utterances which were taken to be divinely inspired by the oracle. Regression may involve a moving back to developmentally earlier feelings, longings, or fears; it may momentarily seem to dissolve long-established boundaries between ourselves and others, inner and outer, subjective and objective, between words and the things they stand for, between thoughts and actions, wishes and events. The regression that is often involved in creative work may make us feel omnipotent, as we did as infants, seeming, with our imagination, to conjure up whatever we wished. It may make us feel as helpless as we did then, when such wishing, a.k.a. "hallucinatory gratification," conjured up nothing we could

39

really use. Regression may bring us to old ways of experiencing ourselves, to feeling out of control or utterly distracted by our preoccu-
pations and inner states.

I told a mentor of an experience I'd had while driving. I was so
preoccupied with a poem I was working on that I apparently failed
to notice a flashing railroad warning light. I crossed the tracks, became aware of a din behind me, glanced in the rearview mirror,
and, yards behind me, saw the passing train. My mentor assured me
that in order to write, one needs to enter such distracted states but,
she cautioned, not at the stove and not in the car. A poet friend,
when I told her, too, about my near encounter with the train, pointed
to the cake she had just brought to the birthday party where we
were talking. It was one of her utterly stunning creations with dark
chocolate shavings, layers of butter cream and genoise. She told me
that in the car en route with her husband, she'd been preoccupied
with an image when she suddenly discovered that the cake had slid
from her lap, gone over her knees, and was slipping rapidly toward
her ankles and the floor. Only by a deft, last-minute flexing of both
feet had she managed to save her culinary creation from disaster.
Even those of us who enjoy such preoccupied and regressed states
enjoy them more at some times than at others, enter them at greater
or at lesser risk, depending on our circumstances and our overall
physical and emotional state.

James Joyce (Ellman, 1959/1982) consulted Carl Jung about his
psychotic daughter. Joyce knew quite a bit about the regions of the
mind he'd had to enter in order to write his brilliant stream of
consciousness, and he knew that this realm had something in common with the psychoses. He asked Jung how he, Joyce, and his daughter differed. Both could dip into what Freud called "primary process
thinking," those regions we enter when we dream and may enter
when we write. Jung said, in essence, you dive, she sinks. Okay, Joyce
may have thought, but probably didn't, what's to guarantee I won't
sink one of these times, too?

A science writer had always wanted but feared to write fiction.
Her emotional life had probably been saved by reading novels, which
she had done throughout her lonely childhood. She read voraciously
also as an adult though her life was much fuller now and less lonely.
She had been left, at the age of 6 months, with a nurse, for somewhere between three months and a year, while her actress mother,
accompanied by her father, worked in another city. During this time,
she never saw her parents. She had no idea until therapy that this
experience had affected her, and she was surprised and moved by
my taking this aspect of her history very seriously indeed.

Some months into the therapy, she had an experience that astonished her. She was describing a twilight state the evening before

when everything seemed to fill with a kind of fog. She had found herself wanting to reach her arms up high, though she didn't know toward what. As she told me about this, she suddenly thought of her father and was surprised to be overcome by feelings of painful longing. It was difficult for her to imagine that these had anything to do with either parent, but certainly not with the father she was sure had never been more to her than the distant figure she remembered from her adolescence. Yet as she spoke, she found herself again wanting to reach up longingly toward something and thought of him. When I said that she seemed to be longing for him to pick her up, the ache and sorrow she felt overwhelmed and frightened her. She again had the sensation from the evening before of being engulfed in fog. She occasionally referred back to this moment during the therapy, but never returned to the experience.

It was shortly after this that she spoke for the first time of having always wanted to write fiction. In the next session, she reported that to her astonishment, she had sat down over the weekend and drafted a short story. Though pleased with both the experience and the result, she said she hadn't liked something about the state she'd found herself in while writing; it was too much like "going back into that fog." It became clear that for her to write anything but the scientific articles she did professionally threatened her with the experience of regression. This she could not tolerate—it felt too "spooky, out of control"—even if preventing herself from experiencing such states meant that the first story she'd surprised herself by writing might also be the last. For her, the experience of regression, which was somehow associated with language and story-telling, seemed to bring her too close to the traumatic states of helplessness and longing from her early childhood. She could derive pleasure and comfort from reading what others wrote when they entered the regions of their imagination, but couldn't risk contact with her own.

Such reactions may be what Ogden (1989, pp. 67–68) has in mind when he writes, partly quoting Tustin, of the fears associated with the "autistic–contiguous mode" of experiencing, that mode from very early in our lives when we begin to feel that our experience is bounded within our bodies in relationship to the body or bodies by which we are first held and touched. He describes the anxiety associated with this "mode" as involving "the experience of impending disintegration of one's sensory surface or one's 'rhythm of safety' resulting in the feeling of leaking, dissolving, disappearing, or falling into shapeless unbounded space . . ." (pp. 67–68). He also refers to this condition as one of "nameless dread." This does seem to describe my patient's experience of the regression that brought her into contact with so early and traumatic a state, so intolerable a reminder of something from her own history, that she would rather never write another piece of fiction than risk going there again.

In contrast to the terror this woman felt in the face of "the fog," I was interested to observe the very different responses to regression of a group of approximately 80 poets and fiction writers. These were master of fine arts students and faculty, gathered for 10 days on a college campus. The occasion was the beginning of a semester in a "low intensive residency" program which allows students to enroll, be physically present for this interval, then do a semester's work by mail with a faculty advisor. I was a student in the program and attended six such 10-day residencies during which students and faculty lived in dorms, ate together in the cafeteria, spent intensive hours in classes, lectures, workshops, conferences, and readings, dealing with emotionally charged material and with interactions about their own and each others' work.

Under conditions which, we would joke, resembled optimal ones for brainwashing—lack of privacy, and often of sleep, removal from familiar surroundings, routines, and roles, from home, family, and friends—the regressive pulls were intense. It was openly acknowledged, including by faculty, that probably everyone at some point during the 10 days, would feel emotionally labile and disoriented, and possibly also overwhelmed, defenseless, vulnerable, and disconnected from the important grounding and orienting aspects of their adult lives. Symptoms were likely to include insomnia, sudden bouts of weeping or laughing, wandering about with a sense of having lost one's moorings, and with regressed feelings of insecurity, confusion, and self-doubt.

These "students" tended to be high functioning adults with careers and families. They included university professors, a college dean, lawyers, physicians, freelance writers, journalists, psychologists, painters and musicians, a television producer, entrepreneurs, and students simultaneously doing graduate work at other institutions. The faculty were all accomplished writers and highly professional, dedicated teachers as well. Students and faculty were either poets or fiction writers or both. That is, all were people for whom the capacity to tolerate and make use of regression is an essential prerequisite for successful work, and an essential and familiar component of their writing lives.

In striking contrast to my patient, with her terror of the engulfing fog, this group of writers seemed, generally, to find the regressed states the residency induced to be wearing, but no cause for alarm. I observed little embarrassment, though there seemed to be more, or at least more reticence to discuss the matter, among the men than the women. I observed several scenes and participated in a few in which a weeping or giddy person was gently, at times hilariously, reassured by others that they, too, had been there, or would be before the residency was over.

At breakfast during one residency, several of us, hesitantly at first, then with candor and humor, described the fantasies we had found ourselves having, some for the first time since high school, about how others viewed us. These included that there had been a gathering the night before to which we alone had not been invited. This was because we were too boring or stupid or tall or short, because our workshop secretly hated our poems or stories, or couldn't forgive us for some insipid remark we had made. Furthermore, our newly assigned supervisor was back in his or her dorm at this very moment pondering how to get us assigned, and fast, to someone else.

The conversation was conducted with a clear mixture of pain and relief. It was clear on this and many other occasions that the capacity to be relatively unalarmed by and open about such states was more widespread, and the experience of regression generally more easily tolerated, than I can imagine its having been in most settings. What may be most significant is that this regression, and the group's tolerance of it, went on in the context of, but did not interfere with, hard work, dedication, discipline, and intellectual rigor required of both students and faculty throughout 9 of the residency's 10 days.

This group of writers has been highly productive and successful if one measures their productivity and success by the number of books they have published, and the literary honors and prizes they have won (Bruck, 1997). They exemplify the fact that flexibility in relationship to regression—Kris' "functional regression," or "regression in the service of the ego" (1964, p. 177)—is a prerequisite for creativity. Such flexibility may also be a prerequisite for emotional health. Conversely, an inability to tolerate the regression that is part of creative work, would constitute an important source of resistance or block.

Even experienced writers like those at the residences know moments of uneasiness at the levels of preoccupation, the giving over of control that such work can require. There are many reasons for this uneasiness, and the resistance or avoidance which can result. For one, the regression that creativity requires involves an easing or reversing of the process whereby we have worked to impose some measure of order on ourselves, have submitted to certain standards of control over our feelings, bodily functions, and thoughts (Milner, 1957, p. 156). If that control was hard won, is tenuous or rigid, or needs continuously to be maintained, then regressed states in which the control must be given up or eased can threaten and make us anxious. It is precisely anxiety which can cause us, automatically, to call upon defensive strategies, including the avoidance of creative work, the sabotaging of a particular poem, article, or book.

Immersing ourselves in language and its rhythms may give us great pleasure, but such immersion, itself a regression, can itself make us anxious. This is so in part because we learn language and hear its rhythms in the context of our earliest relationships. Language and its rhythms, then, can themselves exert regressive pulls. For example, because language is embedded in the early mother–child interaction, the child's, or later the adult's utterance can conjure up parental presences (Loewald, 1980b, p. 180).

Such presences often please and even comfort us. At times of severe trauma, children, especially, may summon such presences by singing to themselves, uttering familiar, repetitive rhymes, or "whistling in the dark" (Terr, 1984, pp. 663–665). The toddler who, some years ago, tumbled into a deep well in Texas and whose difficult, protracted, but ultimately successful rescue was followed by millions through the media, reportedly spent much of her time in the well quietly repeating nursery rhymes to herself while her parents called to her from the surface far above. Greenson (1978) reports the World War II case of a young American soldier drowning in gasoline fumes in a disabled plane who heard, almost like a hallucination, a series of seeming nonsense syllables endlessly, but soothingly, repeated. He was rescued and later consulted with Greenson, and investigation revealed these sounds, which persisted almost ceaselessly for a time after the rescue, to have been a fragment of a Flemish lullaby. The soldier's mother, who had been Belgian and had died when he was 18 months of age, must once have sung it to him. In that near-death experience, he had somehow managed to call forth it, and her. A 12-year-old boy who spent a terrifying 30 minutes outside a fast food restaurant, lying in a pile of bodies, including that of his best friend, while inside the gunman continued the slaughter, later reported that he had quietly sung to himself while lying there, hoping to be rescued. In each of these instances, the singing, whether of nursery rhymes or of an unconsciously stored lullaby, "held" and comforted a person during a terrifying ordeal. It was, for the boy and the soldier, at least, a kind of regressive evocation of the parent's voice that helped to comfort and psychologically to protect at a time of massive trauma.

Language, and especially rhythmic language, can also seem threatening because of precisely this power it has to make us feel like small children again, a power we may fear and resist. If we cannot accept that creative work sometimes involves "surrender, not control" (Hillman, 1988, personal communication), and, indeed, it is a form of surrender we are talking about here, we may need to avoid such work or allow ourselves to do it only occasionally, under certain very safe circumstances or in small increments.

Regression involves a kind of letting go of control, a sense of relaxation or release. Whether such an experience is acceptable or tolerable to an individual will depend on the unconscious meanings he or she ascribes to it (Leader, 1991, quoting Schafer, 1958, pp. 79–80). Where those meanings make the experience feel dangerous, blockage, or at least slowage, of creative work may be inevitable. Milner (1957, p. 156) notes that letting attention suffuse the whole body, as she found herself doing when she painted, and as one does in being receptive to and engaged in creative work, is related to the experience of orgasm. If sexuality and sexual release are areas of conflict, such conflict may make this "suffused attention" feel intolerable.

In writing of rhythm, that essential element in poetry as well as in music, dance, and, perhaps less obviously, the visual arts, Hass (1984) suggests another way in which fear of regression may mobilize anxiety and so contribute to difficulty doing creative work. He discusses rhythm's regressive nature and contrasts that with its progressive, even revolutionary one. His stated intent is not to consider what frightens us in the creative process, but he does suggest that arts which draw on rhythm, as perhaps they all do, present not only pleasure and excitement but also a threat. The threat lies in part in our regressive response to repetitive rhythms which create in us a sense of *dedifferentiation,* of merger with others—the tribal drums that incite to group action, the rhythmic hymns to which the congregation rises as if of one body. Surely this regressive aspect of rhythm is part of its appeal and of the arts of which rhythm is an essential element, but this is also part of what can frighten with its regressive power and pull. This regressive aspect of rhythm can make us feel as one, feel the loss of boundaries between ourselves and others, feel the loss of self in the aggregate, and of course live, for the moment of feeling it, in our body. Hass further describes how rhythm can be arousing, especially new rhythms or variations in familiar ones. Both Hass and Milner (1957, p. 97) note that repetitive rhythm can represent death. Milner adds that it can also represent an imposed, resented order. It shouldn't be difficult, then, to imagine some of the ways in which regression, and the rhythms which express or help bring it about, can make us anxious and potentially interfere with our doing our own creative work, or enjoying the work of others.

Rhythm may be associated with even earlier psychic states than the dedifferentiated one in which the self seems lost in the other. Ogden (1989), in discussing the "autistic–contiguous position," writes:

Contiguity of surfaces (e.g., "molded" skin surfaces, harmonic sounds, rhythmic rocking or sucking, symmetrical shapes) generate the experience of a sensory surface rather than the feeling of two surfaces coming together either in mutually differentiating opposition or in merger. There is practically no sense of inside and outside or self and other; rather, what is important is the pattern, boundedness, shape, rhythm, texture, hardness, softness, warmth, coldness, and so on. (p. 33)

To have sensations which are associated with our first ways of being in the world will involve regressive feelings which sometimes comfort, sometimes frighten us. As Ogden observes, some people shut themselves off to this entire dimension of experience, but they do so at their peril because access to this level of experience is necessary for emotional richness and depth. If creative work requires that we sometimes enter such regressive states, and if for some, or for all at certain times, such entering elicits anxiety, even terror, we can clearly see how fear of regression would be one source of resistance or block. We can see also that access to this level or dimension of experience is an important part of the capacity to do or to enjoy creative work.

A few years ago, I attended a performance of a group called the Drummers of Burundi, shortly before that group's nation was plunged into war. The rhythms became almost oppressively repetitive, the drummers shifted their positions repeatedly, in a choreographed manner that began to suggest their interchangeability, their existence not as individuals but as parts of the aggregate. The rhythms, too, suggested a collective and mounting excitement, nearly orgiastic, with no individual voice. The rising excitement as the soon all too familiar rhythms increased, inexorably it seemed, in pace and volume, finally suggested to me that what Ravel's *Bolero* is to love, this performance was to war. It was a version of foreplay in which the dramatized interchangeability of the musicians, the repetitive but mountingly exciting and excited beat, would serve to move both musicians and listeners at least to imagined or felt action. Here the action being represented was not erotic, as in *Bolero,* but aggressive. This was not about aggression by one person against another. These rhythms seemed rather to suggest a prelude and perhaps even an inducement to group violence, and the performance seemed to have been composed and choreographed with that effect in mind.

There are, then, many things we may resist when we resist the regressive experiences involved in creative work. We may be threatened by the sense of being taken over, or by the power that rhythm seems to have for us and for others. We may need, for example, to resist the kind of experience the Drummers of Burundi seemed to create for their audience, of being appropriated by something in which our very individuality seemed potentially threatened or swallowed up.

Loewald (1980b, pp. 189–199) has noted also that our relationship to the person from whom we learned a word may play a significant role in how alive is the link for us between that word and the thing for which it stands. Our sense, therefore, of the aliveness or deadness of words, our relationship to using them, will be influenced by this aspect of our history. Language also has a magical, evocative aspect. Loewald quotes Valéry, who refers to the spell of poetry, the momentary state where sound and sense are inextricable, and Mallarmé on the "secret parity between old methods of magic and poetry." Loewald is suggesting that the word may have the power to conjure up what it represents, as we have seen it can conjure up the parent and some of the parent's early power to comfort and protect. The word can therefore please, dazzle, or frighten us. Loewald goes on to describe how words may also "embody in the sensory-motor medium what they signify." He means, I believe, that we may *feel* what words stand for in the experience we have of saying or hearing them said. This may lend to words and sentences the aspect of concrete acts or entities, and so cause them to have an even greater regressive power over us. The writer may feel like a magician about to let loose his dangerous and seductive powers. Of course, he may also feel impotent in the face of language that refuses. Sadoff (1991, personal communication) has said, "You can no more make a poem work than you can make someone love you." We may resist the regression inherent in both sets of feelings, of power and of powerlessness.

Paradoxically, we seem to need to give in to these regressive aspects of creativity if we are to experience the ways in which doing creative work affords us an exhilarating discovery of our truest, most separate, and distinctive self. We must blur the boundaries, give up some measure of control to find what is distinctively our own. If we are too frightened to experience our own version of that fog my patient described, our attempts to discover what is new or meaningful will be made more difficult. We will be trying, at great cost to our creativity, to control the process when we should be allowing it, at least initially, to unfold in whatever ways it will.

5

OTHER RESISTANCES: A MISCELLANY

Resistance may also be based on our transference to the reader or viewer; that is, on our unconscious expectations, ideas, and fantasies about the known or imagined others who will see our work. We are inevitably influenced by such others with the power we bestow on them to praise, love, accept, or reject us. Their approbation, censure, envy, admiration, or desire, as we unconsciously imagine it, can sustain or make us anxious and so influence us at any point along the way. Though we are generally unaware of these transferences as we work, the ease or difficulty with which we proceed, the pleasure or panic we experience, can surely alert us to their presence, perhaps even their shape. Such transferences vary for the same writer or artist with different subject matter and in different emotional states. Several may be present as we work, some helpful, some a hinderance. I suspect they have kinship with muses. Certainly they influence what we write and write about, much as the therapist, the actual person and the person as seen through the lens of transference, helps determine what the patient speaks of, thinks about, and even dreams.

At a writers' conference, I was intrigued by what appeared to be the participants' intense and in some instances almost instantaneous transference reactions to the faculty, particularly those with whom participants were to work. One faculty member, when I spoke to him about this, said he had been unsettled by some of the reactions he was encountering and had encountered in comparable situations elsewhere. Those he taught would become intensely attached to him, treat his word as gospel, or fight him as if he were the father of their adolescence. They would attribute to him the power to discern, even to determine, their ultimate fate as artists. They would hunger for his attention, advice, approval, and love. This was, no doubt, in part a response to his stature as a poet, his personality and teaching style, but more significantly the reactions he described seemed to be an instant transference to the desired and feared reader of the participants' work. The respective ages of faculty and conference participants—both groups were adults, with the students often older than faculty—did no more to mitigate these reactions than do such reality factors in psychotherapy or psychoanalysis.

Students in writing programs often notice their work changing as they change teachers. This may be a function not only of the learning process and the writer's development over time, but also of feelings, perhaps unconscious ones, about whether the reader or teacher is male or female, the imagined source of censure, validation, or love. During one semester of my M.F.A. program, I found myself, suddenly and for the first time, writing about adolescent sexuality. During another, themes of absent or disappointing men began to pervade my work. During a third, my poems became more lush and complex than before, and more mysterious. There were, from one semester and teacher to the next, shifts also in the nature and extent of the risks I found myself taking as a writer. The influences which determined these choices and changes were myriad; I'm certain that one influence was my sense of each reader, including not only fair, accurate assessments, but also those less rational, less conscious judgments and reactions, or transferences, that I had and that we all have to each person who plays an important role in our lives.

It isn't difficult then to imagine our transferences to unknown, imagined readers of as yet unwritten work, or work in progress; to invisible editors, with their power to accept or reject that work, as well as to critics, audiences, or reviewers. Such transferences can inspire hope, fear, and dread, get in the way of the work or help it along at every phase.

Transference expectations can be based on actual past experiences with important people in our lives, or on how we interpret, misinterpret, or revise those experiences. Our expectations can be based also on feelings, impulses, or desires we project (i.e., attribute to others because we can't bear to recognize or acknowledge them as our own). The problem is that what we project onto others, we then anticipate or fear at their hand, a point I will expand on in chapter 7. Such projections are not rare and can cause us to experience the imagined other in ways that make us feel vulnerable. In fact we may feel too vulnerable to create, or to expose what we have made to the anticipated ridicule, aggression, contempt, envy, or whatever else we've tried, through projection, to repudiate in ourselves.

Positive responses from others may also be feared if these are felt to be dangerous. The admiration we may imagine we have elicited, or the desire, can frighten us. We may worry that with success will come envy, though the envy we most fear may be our (projected) own. We may fear others' imagined excitement and our responses to it. Such attributions to the outside world or to the imagined reader can be important, problematical sources of anxiety and resistance because, like the other resistances I have described, these can be unconscious and so detected only by their effects on us. Such effects may manifest themselves at any point, from a work's inception, to its being offered to editors, readers, and critics.

Resistance can be mobilized because the writer or artist fears the feelings creative work evokes in her or may reveal. Such fears can occur in response to positive as well as to negative feelings. Joy, elation, or excitement, experiencing ourselves as powerful, admirable, or desirable can frighten us. We may imagine that if we have such feelings, we will alienate others, and make them envy or reject us. We may fear that our immersion in creative work will make us forget others, and so hurt or lose them.

Our feelings may threaten to overwhelm us, leaving us helpless and vulnerable. Milner (1957, ch. 5) has described the fears we may experience of the intensity involved in transforming the outer, and no doubt also the inner, world into images which convey its richness, an intensity which we may feel threatens us with madness. Milner notes, too, that those aspects of the external world to which the artist attends may feel like the exact embodiment of what she hungers for and so seem to call into question her existence as a separate being. Resistances to strong feelings and to the dangers they seem to pose may occur in conjunction with any of the other resistances I have described.

The patient in psychotherapy or psychoanalysis is helped to feel relatively safe in relationship to the emergence of strong feelings and charged material by the therapeutic relationship and by those aspects of the therapeutic situation we refer to as "the frame." What is said is confidential, what is wished or felt will not, generally, be judged, or acted upon. Virtually anything can be said without dangerous consequences. There is a known time and place within which the relationship and the material unfold. The patient is safely "held" where regression is permitted, even fostered, and does not actually expose him or her to danger. Rothenberg (1979, pp. 351–357), in his study of creativity, suggests that there are analogous, reassuring elements in the creative process. The anxiety mobilized by the creative person's approach to conflictual material is mitigated or made manageable by the gradual emergence of the artist's themes, by the form or structure of the work of art, by the process as the artist comes to trust it, and by "progressive mastery." Not everyone who wants to do creative work, however, knows or trusts these aspects of the process and how they help with the management of strong feelings, and so they may fear the process too greatly to be able to proceed.

Hamer (1995) has described his experience writing a poem on the painful and charged subject of racism. The poem was triggered by his being picked up, not for the first time, by the police, shoved into a police car in front of neighbors, and questioned about a robbery, merely because, like the robber in question, he is a tall black man and was wearing a light colored jacket. He has described how the writing of that poem occurred slowly, over weeks, in manageable steps or doses, allowing him to find the form, images, and music his subject required, and making his approach to the difficult feelings of rage and humiliation tolerable enough, much as Rothenberg suggested, for him to be able to use them in the poem. Hamer was able to trust in his own creative process despite the difficulties with which this poem confronted him. One who lacks trust in the process or his ability to cope with strong and difficult feelings, may be less able to let the work unfold as Hamer describes.

Resistance to strong feelings may manifest itself in the avoidance of specific details in a work when the details are associated with, or seem to contain, those feelings. Such avoidance often occurs, and for similar reasons, in psychotherapy or analysis. For example, an artist I was seeing in therapy, whose ability to describe was excellent, was talking about having bought herself something. Her reluctance to buy herself beautiful things, though she loved and could afford them, had been an important expression of her feeling undeserving and of her fear of being like her mother, whom she considered shallow and greedy. I said she was being uncharacteristically vague about what the purchase had been. This irritated her; she thought it trivial and feared I was indulging some frivolous curiosity of my own in making the observation. Then she began, at first compliantly, to describe the purchase of a quilt handmade from pieces of antique fabric. Suddenly she began to cry. The beauty of the piece had moved her, as had her newfound willingness to give to herself. In the past, she would have waited for someone else, usually her mother, to do so and then inevitably been disappointed. She was surprised at the intense feelings that emerged from her description, then wondered whether she should be. She knew from her art and her therapy that for her, focusing on specificity of detail or on an image often gave her access to her most important feelings and generated some of her best work.

We learned she had started off being vague about details because she feared that if she told me what she had, she'd become emotional about her purchase and I'd think her frivolous or shallow. Underlying this was a fear I would envy her as her mother apparently had. Then, as the envious do, I would try to spoil her pleasure. This discovery, that she had withheld the details in order to fend off her own delight and excitement and to avoid my envy, led to productive work on how her fear of being envied also kept her from showing her art. Only when we considered her resistance to discussing specific details did we get at these important conflicts, feelings, and fantasies.

The writer who is vague or suddenly becomes so may similarly be manifesting resistance to frightening or exciting feelings, wishes, or fantasies which a clearer rendering of an image, a more careful word choice might reveal. This form of resistance, expressed by avoidance of specificity of image or detail, can weaken, even ruin a work. So, of course, can excessive or rigid use of detail, which may also be defensive.

Resistance to feelings can manifest itself in other ways. I wrote an unsatisfying poem about the imagined items lost in ivy, a poem I knew, but knew only generally, had to do with loss. Among the nondistinctive keys, coins and tennis balls which the ivy in the poem concealed, there appeared a to me mysterious watch. It had a textured, brown leather band, a narrow, rectangular yellowed face, black roman numerals, and a cracked crystal. A mentor, noting the specificity of this one image, and how it stood out from the rest, said, "This watch wants a poem of its own."

When I wrote that poem, after months of obsessing, even dreaming, about watches, a subject not generally of interest to me, I had a better piece of work than in the ivy poem and uncovered a lost piece of my childhood which psychoanalysis had failed to discover. The watch, "forgotten" for decades, had been a seventh birthday present. I had broken it in a fall by a pond that autumn, shortly after my parents each lost a parent, went into mourning, and for a time became emotionally unavailable. I'd had a slight amnesia for this period and had, for years, become mildly depressed in autumn. I experienced this "return of the repressed," wrote the stronger poem, and ceased to have my heretofore inexplicable autumn depressions. All this became possible because the blandness of my ivy poem and the contrasting specificity in it of the watch had caught the attention of a smart reader who, like a good therapist, noticed where the language was alive and invited me to go there.

Resistance, then, in creative work, as in therapy, can reveal itself in the avoidance of specificity of detail, like my patient's, or mine in most of my ivy poem, or in sudden, contrasting specificity, which the attuned reader, or therapist, will notice as likely to be signaling the presence of a concealed emotional hot spot. The writer or artist needs to be attuned to such signs in the work or have a good reader, or therapist, who calls attention to them. Like the sudden, insistent dipping of the dowser's stick, such signs can alert us to the proximity, even the location, of what we seek.

Sometimes resistance manifests itself not in paucity or dullness of detail, the sudden contrasting appearance of vivid language or a striking image. Instead there are changes in one's usual style, abrupt, inexplicable shifts in levels of diction—shifts that serve no apparent artistic purpose. Language may become clichéd in a writer from whom this is unexpected, become uncharacteristically reticent, or go flat.

We encounter such signs often in therapy where we need certainly to notice them. The generally candid patient, like my artist, alludes to something but suddenly avoids specifics. She becomes vague about where she went or what she did. Or, although, when speaking of others, she typically refers to them by name, she now goes into syntactical thickets to avoid doing so. A patient's diction shifts, seemingly inexplicably, from one level or style to another: The individual who is generally blunt and uses germanic rather than latinate English words—is more likely to say "fucked" than "had sexual intercourse," "shit" rather than "feces"—suddenly uses the more latinate, formal versions of English. The person whose speech tends to be informal suddenly sounds as if he or she were addressing the Supreme Court. The generally articulate adult lapses into childhood forms of speech, makes untypical childlike errors in grammar or diction. The typically engaging patient becomes soporific; the therapist becomes aware of a sudden longing to sleep.

When we call such shifts in people's use of language to their attention and inquire about them, in therapy and in writers' workshops, or attend to our own such shifts, something useful is likely to happen. Previously submerged feelings, thoughts, memories, wishes, or fantasies may surface; dead spots may be cut away, allowing poem, story, or hour to come alive; the hot spot is fanned and ignited. Our important material can be made accessible. Both writers and therapists do well to notice such indications, in the language, of signs that resistance is operating and restricting the work. Parallels exist in other media—for painters, in their effective or ineffective use of color, form, or composition, for sculptors in the motion or stasis of their materials and forms, for choreographers in the aliveness or deadness of given movements in a dance.

Resistance in creative endeavors may also result from conscious or unconscious concerns about what we reveal or expose. Pinsky (1988) told a poetry workshop that to write, you have to be willing to make a fool of yourself. If we're unable to risk this, at least to risk doing it voluntarily, to subject our thoughts, feelings, abilities, or lack thereof, to scrutiny, we hobble ourselves in creative work. Such hobbling may result not only from a fear of looking foolish; it may also have to do with a need to protect others.

I asked two widely published poets how they deal with personal material, the divulging of which could hurt people in their lives. I reminded them that therapists, when we write about clinical work, face a related question. How can we responsibly disguise certain subject matter and protect our patients from feeling exploited or exposed, but disguise and protect without doing violence to the essay, book, or, in some instances, the poem.

Both poets had grappled with this question and arrived at different answers for themselves. One said that if the material is emotionally true, he feels he has the right to use it. The other, perhaps because what he has written is more likely to have distressed people close to him, said his solution had been to wait until the subject of some of his poems had died before he published them. This enabled him to write freely and protect her from the pain of having him reveal his view of her. Knowing this was to be his plan from the first had freed him to write the poems since they could be true to his experience and intent, but not do harm.

A third poet told me that like many of her contemporaries, she treats distressing personal material as if it were not autobiographical. She writes using *personae* or masks, or writes as if certain of her experiences, feelings, and states belonged to mythical, historical, or anonymous figures or events. It is not the poet's father who has betrayed his daughter, but Iphegenia's. And sometimes, she added, she publishes under a pseudonym.

A poet friend knew I was having difficulty writing. She knew, too, that I was struggling with troubling feelings about someone I needed and wanted to protect. She suggested that my difficulty in writing—everything I did at the time seemed polite and flat—might have to do with fears of exposing what I felt to be my own awfulness for having my feelings and thoughts, and of hurting this person I loved by revealing them. She suggested I write about what I felt and imagined, but plan to show what I wrote to no one, plan even to burn it, or send it to her to store for me, or bury in her yard.

My first attempts were awful, but I persisted and began to feel I'd written my way out of the stuckness. I couldn't seem to write anything worthwhile about what had been troubling me, but I did start to be able to write again about other matters. Then, months later, I returned to the difficult subject and wrote what for me was a breakthrough poem. It was one of the best things I'd done and dealt with my subject in a manageable but effective way. I found that I was comfortable publishing the poem in a review and later an anthology under my own name. The object of my difficult feelings later came across the poem, read it, and was neither hurt nor offended, perhaps because the feelings had, by the time they informed that poem, been transmuted into metaphor. My friend's proposed solution proved helpful. Without it, I might neither have written the successful poem nor written anything else for some time. That this particular resistance was conscious no doubt made it easier to overcome.

We may experience resistance at any point along the way. We may have trouble getting started, continuing, revising, or completing the work. We may run into problems submitting it, or going on to the next thing. We may have difficulty with any of these steps because of the various anxieties and resistances I have mentioned or because of others having to do with our particular relationship to writing or making art.

Some find getting started especially difficult. Writers describe rituals they go through before they sit down to write, which serve in part to allay the anxiety that getting started can mobilize. Hugo (1979, p. 3) advises the student writer to sharpen "about 20" number 2 pencils as a way to begin. An acquaintance, whose work I and many others admire, told me of promising himself two chocolate chip cookies if he wrote for two hours. An M.F.A. classmate of mine needed, and was fortunate enough to be able to afford, two hours each day of wandering about before she settled down to work. The anxieties about starting will vary. We may fear finding nothing there, or finding too much that is rich and exciting, discovering parts of the self that are ugly, encountering any of the other difficulties I have described, and no doubt some I haven't.

I've considered the problems we encounter when we revise in chapter 3, but want to add that revision may be resisted because it can feel like, or be seen by others as being, a kind of madness, a compulsion, when we work for hours, days, or weeks on a word or line, or on getting a color right.

A colleague seeing a painter in therapy, told me about listening to the painter describe the hours he had spent trying to get a precise shade of blue. The therapist, who was not an artist, told me he was puzzled at first and heard the effort and the painter's persistance as compulsive, as a defense, albeit not characteristic for this patient, against something the artist unconsciously experienced as dangerous or unacceptable. My colleague went on listening, however, trying to understand, and finally realized that the painter was working to get an exact feeling, experience, state of mind, or sense of the physical world onto his canvas and that for him, only the precise shade of blue would accomplish this. Anyone unable to appreciate what may be at stake in such an effort may want to read Heinrich Wiegand Petzet's Preface to Rilke's *Letters on Cezanne* (Rilke, 1985) or the book itself. When my colleague stopped thinking about the effort as defensive or pathological and began to recognize what was at stake for the artist in the painting he was able to better understand his artist patient and perhaps the creative process as well. For the painter it was a piece of self-discovery, a communication with others, the creating of something important, perhaps essential. An artist needs to recognize this for himself. If he pathologizes what revision may involve, or getting the color right, as this therapist initially did, the artist may compound the difficulty he faces and sabotage his work.

Endless revising *can* be an expression of resistance or indicative of psychopathology. Consider the book that is worked on for decades, not because it keeps getting better, but because its author requires an unachievable perfection or control. Or the painting that is perpetually in progress because the painter can't bear to accept what he can't make happen. If we refuse to recognize that point at which we've carried the work as far as we can and need to let it go, our work will have become not creative, but compulsive.

Finishing has charged emotional meanings beyond confronting us with imperfection in the life or in the work. To finish may feel like an entrapment. We may fear we'll be stuck within the confines of what we've made and so need to keep it going. Endlessly. The artist who feels this way may resemble the woman who built the Winchester Mystery House in California. Perhaps believing that when that house was finished, she would die, she kept adding to it, constructing stairways to ceilings, doors that opened onto walls.

To finish may represent growing up and leaving home. Dissertations come to mind. To finish may stand for killing off our parents as we demonstrate that we are no longer small and dependent on them, or that we have surpassed them in ways that may concern us (see chapter 6). Where finishing has such meanings, and such meanings are conflictual, resistance may well be mobilized in response. The prospect of finishing can also mobilize resistance if, consciously or unconsciously, finishing represents mortality. Closure does have such associations, which may help to account for some of the writers, and others, who never finish things, take forever to finish, or finish only with great difficulty. Finishing may also feel like the giving up of something one wishes to hold onto in a retentive, but pleasurable way.

Finishing, or achieving closure in creative work, has its counterpart, albeit inexact, in the finishing of therapeutic hours and the terminations of therapies or analyses. Often at termination, as at closure, there are poignant mixtures of appreciation, a sense of accomplishment, frustration and anger at what hasn't been achieved, disappointment, pleasure, hope for whatever is next, a sense on both sides of the loss of an intense and important relationship, and of involvement in a process. In the creative context, the loss is of the unique relationship with that particular creation, and perhaps also with any mentor, or others who have played a part. Just as the wish to be spared these feelings may cause patients in therapy to end prematurely or abruptly, or be reluctant to end at all, so may a wish to be spared such feelings cause creative work to be left unfinished or to be finished precipitously.

Herrnstein Smith (1968, sec. 5, ch. 2, 3), in discussing poetic closure, says that closure may be "strong" or "weak." Strong closure gives a sense of finality; the work seems to "click shut." This may be accomplished through imagery, structure, sound, rhyme scheme, or some combination of these. Weak closure leaves us with a sense of something open-ended, unresolved, something we may return to, and for which we may imagine different outcomes, a sort of poetic ellipsis. Herrnstein Smith makes clear that "strong" and "weak" in this context are not value judgments. Different poems, poets, and eras call for closures of different kinds.

Though Herrnstein Smith is writing about the poems themselves and not the writer's experience of them or the process whereby they came to be made, what she says is relevant here. Some writers can't achieve strong closure in their relationship to the work, others can't tolerate the ambiguity inherent in weak closure, though the ambiguity may be what the work or the process requires. How the artist or writer handles closure will depend on what closure means to her, on what anxieties or resistances finishing involves. We've all known writers, painters, and others who can't finish things, or who finish, then can't go on to the next task, because the sense of loss, the anxiety is too great, or they can't bear to let go.

Two works, similar in structure, play on our responses to closure and the avoidance of it intriguingly: the film, *The Saragossa Manuscript* (Has, 1965) and Italo Calvino's novel *If on a Winter's Night a Traveler* (1981/1979). In both, a story begins, the viewer or reader becomes engaged with it, there is what appears at first to be a digression, a story within a story. In time, the viewer or reader realizes that the first story seems to have been left behind but she is now engrossed in the second. Suddenly this story, too, is interrupted as someone in it begins to tell another story. Soon it is that third story we are engrossed in, having, at first reluctantly, given up the story before. This process continues into a fourth and a fifth story until the reader or viewer experiences a reaction that is an odd mixture of hilarity and anxiety. It becomes clear that no story will have an ending. Closure has been foresworn. There is perhaps a slightly manic quality to this procedure; one thinks of Scheherazade telling stories to the sultan, each night leaving him in suspense so he will spare her life. Endings are delayed so the teller can fend off death. These two works thwart our need for closure, making us aware of the anxiety involved where closure does not occur, or at least closure as we have come to expect it from our literary and film traditions. We vary as to which makes us more anxious, the lack of closure these works insist upon, or closure itself. For some, closure needs to be avoided, the work left unfinished or worked on interminably. The director of *The Saragossa Manuscript* and the author of *If on a Winter's Night a Traveler,* play with these themes, of closure resisted and closure needed, each eliciting, then thwarting our expectations and needs.

Oremland (cited in Bergmann, 1997, p. 192) has suggested that the artist's relationship to his or her art is "an object relationship," an idea I will touch on again in chapter 7. If Oremland is correct, and in part he is, then finishing a piece of work with which we have an intense relationship, as we do with important people in our lives, can certainly involve a sense of loss. The feelings may be mixed, like the ones we experience sending children off to college. If sending what we have been instrumental in creating into the world leaves us feeling more bereft than proud, if we have little else to engage us or a resulting sense of emptiness, then such finishing or closure may be resisted. We may be inclined to linger over our fears for the work's shortcomings and our own. Or the work may be so beloved that we feel disloyal to it in bestowing our attention on the next creation or "child."

We may resist sending work out or showing it because to do so risks rejection, exposure, or success, doing less well than, or better than another. Sending our work out or showing it may represent a giving up of control over that work and its fate, because in doing so we subject it, and ourselves, to the reactions of others. Others' reactions may, as we've seen, be feared because of what we project onto them, or because of the meanings to us of the ways they may respond.

We may resist going on to the next thing, to confronting, once again, the empty canvas or blank page, regardless of whether any previous work we've done was well received. An author whose identity is unknown to me expressed this quite clearly. Apparently, upon being asked whether having had two successful books made it easier for him to start the third, he said, "The third book doesn't know that the other two were written."

I've considered many resistances we may encounter in trying to write or do other creative work. I haven't included all the forms of block or resistance; each writer or artist, if inventive, will invent her own. The forms of resistance I have discussed don't usually exist in isolation from each other, nor is one necessarily always manifest in any individual artist's work. There may be many operating at a time. They may shift, depending on innumerable variables. They may render us incapable of doing art. Or they may be held at bay like a tiger by a skilled and lucky trainer, armed with whip and chair. They may seem to vanish entirely, allowing excellent work to go forward, though no writer or artist with whom I've discussed the matter ever seems convinced they're gone for good.

6

CREATIVITY AND THE STAGES OF PSYCHOLOGICAL DEVELOPMENT

The difficulties with creative work that I have described result from psychological conflict which has roots in early experience and the developmental stages. These stages aren't only a potential source of resistance to or inhibition of creative work, however. They are a source of the artist's themes, her desire and ability to create, and her relationship to her chosen medium. It seems useful, then, in discussing creativity and creative blocks, to consider the developmental stages and how the negotiating of each, with its tasks, challenges, and potentials, can contribute to or interfere with creative work.

Ehrenzweig (1967, pp. xiv, 176–177) notes that the deepest of what he calls the "poemagogic" images, images from mythology and art which are associated with the creative act, represent "the 'oceanic' level where we feel our individual existence lost in mystic union with the universe." While to some, such "union" has religious or mystical implications, in analytic thinking it derives from our earliest relationship with our mother, before we experience ourselves as separate beings. That Ehrenzweig should suggest a link, reflected in myth and art, between creative work and that early experience of oneness, is no surprise. Artists speak of trying to (re)create the experience of wholeness or perfection, as if it had once been theirs, and might, in the creative act, be regained. The regressed, taken-over states, feelings of being swept up, or lost in the creative act, are familiar to poets and others as well. Also familiar is the sensation of serving as a medium for something larger, more powerful, and unseen, of being summoned, seized, or abandoned by the muse.

What are the implications of that first experience of oneness, our longing to recapture it, and the fear that in doing so, we will be drawn back into feeling, wonderfully or terrifyingly, merged or taken over? The implications for pleasure in the making and enjoying of art are easy to discern. They exist in the love of rhythm and sound, which move us in a way we intuit goes back to before we had language, and in our pleasure in pattern, motion, and color. They are to be found in our response to the magical, evocative, incantatory power of words that dates from a time before words became distanced from sensory/bodily experience, the things they stand for, and the people from whom we originally learned them.

For some people, however, the transient regressions to seemingly undifferentiated states that creative work often requires, seem threatening. They fear they will be "reabsorbed" into something or someone else, and they become anxious, perhaps too anxious to proceed. They may feel like the woman, abandoned by her parents during her first year of life (chapter 4), for whom writing fiction proved intolerable because it threatened her with becoming lost irretrievably in the fog.

Where such states are primarily experienced as pleasurable, they may be an incentive to creative work. Many enjoy the intense absorption such work entails, even the momentary blurring of boundaries it often involves. Loewald (1988, p. 33) suggests that rather than being a defense, even a developmentally advanced defense, against more direct expressions of what we deem unacceptable wishes, sublimation, of which creativity is a prime example, is often an expression of our innate and healthy longings for just such unity or wholeness.

In the early months of life the baby's relationship to the world is an oral one, and this, too, has positive and negative implications for the making of art. Infants mouth things as a way of exploring them, are busily involved in sucking, babbling, cooing, gurgling, biting, and spitting up. The world is taken in through the mouth, and also through the eyes, ears, and skin. Taking in may be, and remain, highly pleasurable; learning, reading, listening, looking may all later be sources of delight. What is taken in, however, seems to disappear. The baby, who becomes angry when frustrated, may feel that her anger destroys what she takes in, and that she, and her desires, are therefore bad and dangerous. These angry feelings are later repressed. But they and the accompanying fantasies of her destructiveness may make the baby, later the child or adult, imagine that what she is curious about, wishes to make a part of herself, or otherwise to take in, she thus threatens to destroy. If so, the wish to take in will feel dangerous. The baby may come to fear her own desires, greed, curiosity, and aggression, making it difficult for her later to want things, learn (take in) from others, absorb information, or risk exposing the associated "inner badness" through creative work.

The baby, or small child, even the adult, often deals with such unacceptable feelings and wishes by projecting them onto others—*it's not I who would eat or tear them up; it's they who would do so to me.* The resulting fears may include being attacked, eaten, or otherwise made to disappear, as a perusal of fairy tales like *Little Red Riding Hood* or *Hansel and Gretel,* a familiarity with the monster-in-my-closet fantasies of small children, readily suggests. Such projections make the world seem hostile and can cause us as adults to fear in advance an attack by readers, viewers, critics, and others, onto whom we have similarly projected our hostility, envy, badness, or greed.

Our idioms show how closely linked for us are orality, love, and aggression, and that both loving and aggressive expressions of orality are often imagined to be dangerous. Consider: a biting comment, they chewed him out, they chewed him up and spat him out, he'll eat you for lunch, she tore into him, he bit her head off, you swallowed it whole, just eat it, chew on this, it sticks in my throat, what's eating you, spit it out, they'll eat you alive, he sucked up to them, I could eat you up, you look good enough to eat, she's/he's luscious, yummy, delectable, scrumptious, they hungered for each other, they nibbled at each other, he devoured her with his eyes, they were consumed with desire (jealousy, rage). There are the endearments—honey, cookie, babycakes, sweet thing—which suggest the wish to take in or to devour, and the more subtle, but still telling expressions: what good taste you have, he became bitter, you were always so sweet, she has a thirst/hunger for knowledge, a taste for travel, an appetite for life, we'll need to digest this, he regurgitated the answers, she can't stomach it, he needs to absorb it, we took (couldn't take) it all in.

Most people probably aren't often conscious of fantasies in which their curiosity, desire, greed, and aggression are dangerous, even devouring. They may, however, encounter such fantasies, disguised, in their dreams, and in folklore and art, and there respond to what is at once strange and familiar. Some who do become aware of these early "primitive" fantasies, become anxious, mobilize their defenses, and cease to be so aware. Or they become overwhelmed, fear disorganization, and act the frightening fantasies out. Others will have conscious access to these presumably universal fantasies without apparent difficulty and can symbolically represent them, including in works of art.

Picasso (Fadiman, 1985, p. 452) described lunching daily in a restaurant, near a side table which, one day in his studio, he decided to paint. The next day, when he went to the restaurant, the table was gone. He said, "I must have taken it away without noticing by painting it." It seems he could imagine, even if in jest, that by taking something into himself and making it into art, he made it cease to exist as itself, and could imagine this consciously, without being psychotic, experiencing massive anxiety, or having to shut off contact with his inner life. He had the capacity, that is, for what Kris (1964,

p. 177) called "regression in the service of the ego." He could gain access to the kinds of thinking and perceiving which originate early in life, not be made overly anxious by these, and use them in his work. Consider, for example, his tongues that are also daggers, breasts that look like eyes.

People who can have conscious access to such images or thoughts without alarm and can make creative use of them, can do so for many reasons. Presumably their anxiety is not great, or they have achieved a high enough tolerance for and ability to manage it—a developmental attainment from somewhat later than the stage I am discussing here. Perhaps, also, the artistic or literary forms being used, the creative process when it is approached in tolerable doses, and the ongoing experience of that process, permit mastery (Rothenberg, 1979, pp. 351–357).

It has been suggested that only what we have repressed can be symbolized (Segal, 1991, p. 29). I understand this to mean that we need to be able actively to keep from conscious awareness some of our early aggressive and other frightening feelings and fantasies, if we are to become distanced enough from them to represent them in words or other symbolic forms. Picasso was apparently able to repress whatever feelings or fantasies would otherwise have made those disappearing tables and knife-tongues too frightening for him to imagine them. Both this capacity to repress and the capacity to gain access to early forms of thought and to the images that convey these, are essential to the artist and are influenced by his or her journey through the early stages of development.

During the first months of life, the baby alternatingly feels om-nipotent (she pictures something and it appears; she makes a sound and the desired one comes to her), and painfully, frustratingly help-less (she needs, but has to wait; she is unable to soothe herself or summon up the comfort she needs; she can't control the world out-side of herself, or the world within). Certainly the later attempt to create a world in one's poem, story, or painting can gratify the long-ing, associated with this early stage, and persisting for many through-out life, to recapture a sense of that lost omnipotence. This may be another motivation for doing creative work in which we feel, at moments, as if we were immensely powerful and could repair the damaged world, make of it what we will, and provide ourselves with what we need. But if the inability to make things happen, however much we try, is intolerable, because we know it too well from this early and vulnerable time, if the feelings of lost omnipotence associ-ated with this stage are intolerable, because we too early lost the illusion of power, our creativity may be impaired.

We need, to be able to do such work, to bear the frustration when the words, paint, or whatever won't do our bidding; when the outside world won't meet our needs to have our work welcomed, our efforts loved. Feeling passive or helpless, having to wait for things to unfold, can be painful, because it represents a regression to the difficult feelings of this stage. If such feelings are experienced now as intensely, even traumatically, as they were in early childhood, how much more difficult it will be to do work which at times we can only let come, try to shape, be patient with, persist at, and learn about and from. Alternatively, if doing creative work makes us feel powerful, as it can, and the sense of power terrifies us because we imagine it will lead to destructiveness and loss, we may need to keep that power carefully, perhaps too carefully, in check.

Doing creative work can be an attempt to create one's own "container" for experiences which would otherwise be overwhelming. It can be a way of coping with the barrage of external and internal stimuli which, ideally, the mother, acting as container, first makes it possible for the infant to tolerate and sort out. Golden (1987) suggests that creative work typically serves this purpose for people who, as small children, were routinely overwhelmed by stimuli, either because the environment, usually the mother, lacked the ability to serve as a sufficient container, or because the child's "wiring" (not her word), or temperament, was such that she required a greater container of stimuli than the mother could reasonably provide. Golden says that creativity doesn't necessarily develop to defend or compensate, but that it can have this early motivation or origin. Since artists often tend to be more sensitive to stimuli than others (Greenacre, 1971, p. 485), they may indeed have an innately greater need than most people for an effective container to help them dose and manage their experience. Such a need may be difficult even for quite adequate mothers to meet. I'm not sure there is evidence to suggest as Golden does, however, that where creativity exists to serve as a container, it may do so because of severe or consistent maternal failure.

One young man, whose development I had occasion to follow, early demonstrated the kinds of sensitivities Golden and Greenacre seem to have in mind, and the greater need for a container, though I have no reason to think that there was, in this case, significant maternal failure. As an infant, he was bothered by even minor noises: A passing car, a squeaking floorboard would startle him awake. While he was being breast-fed, he would respond to the presence in the room of any third person with evident distress. He needed to have labels removed from clothing or he would become agitated, apparently at how they felt against his skin. As a toddler he became distraught in crowds or in the presence of even slightly agitated, hurried, or upset persons. At 18 months, the sight of a noticeably depressed but not otherwise remarkable mother at the next swing in the park made him cringe, whimper, and reach for his own mother, as if for protection. At the same age, he reacted intensely to music, sometimes showing great delight, but often sobbing in response to it, as if in grief. Things which others seemed to notice slightly or ignore—a bird flying nearby, a brightly colored sticker—pleased and engaged him intensely.

His parents tried, during his infancy and early childhood, to dose the external stimuli in response to his needs, removing him from crowded places if these agitated him, keeping the noise level low when possible. But they often felt that his needs for protection from what he clearly experienced as too much stimuli from within and without exceeded what they could provide. He did well, however, in response both to their efforts to be attuned to his needs and to psychotherapy for anxiety during his early school years. He became better able to tolerate even high levels of stimuli, including his internal responses to change, which early on overwhelmed him, and to accommodate more flexibly to new experiences than during his first years of life.

By 15, he was a gifted musician and painter, doing well in school both academically and socially. His special sensitivities and accompanying need for greater "containment" did appear to have coincided in his case with special artistic talents. But while Golden might argue that his creative interests, or the ways he used these, resulted from failures of his early environment, I believe that had it failed him significantly in this way, he would have lacked the capacities required to do creative work. While it is clear that his needs for a container were greater than average, and greater than his parents could consistently provide, I believe he identified with their presumably adequate "containing function" and learned in this way to provide himself with what he needed. He would go to his music or painting at times of distress or in the face of other internal and external pressures and come away sometimes calmed, sometimes happily excited and gratified by what he was able so effectively to create.

Rothenberg's observation (1979, pp. 351–357) that the forms the artist uses and the process as she learns to let it unfold help to contain the anxiety that creative work inevitably mobilizes, is salient here. Perhaps Rothenberg, too, is suggesting that one function of creative work is to serve as a container for experience. The person whose need for containment early in life was unmet, however, may be unable to manage the anxiety that is inevitably a part of any creative activity or to sense that the process may provide containment.

Another aspect of early development with significance for the making of art is the baby's use of transitional objects and transitional phenomena (Winnicott, 1951/1971a). If all goes well, the baby's teddy bear or blanket becomes a transitional object. It stands for the mother, because the baby imbues it with the power she has to soothe, but it stands also for the baby's inner world. It helps to effect a transition between external reality and how it is represented internally, between the objective and the subjective worlds. The transitional object also is a step on the baby's way to being able to soothe herself and so helps in the developmental process of separation-individuation. If the mother is lost too early—dies, is depressed, preoccupied, or too long absent—the power and worth of the transitional object will be lost as well. It will lose its power and worth because, while it partially stands for the mother, it does not replace her. Where the relationship survives, the transitional object continues to soothe in the mother's absence, for as long as it is needed. It is also used when the baby needs to withdraw from the mother, as she may while holding the blanket or bear, and with it, comforting or soothing herself to sleep.

In time, the transitional object loses its meaning and is given up. Its meaning, or function spreads across a wider field. That meaning or function is to provide and stand for an intermediate experience between inner and outer, between subjectivity, which at its extreme is madness, and objectivity, which at its extreme is a cold, meaningless world. The wider field includes transitional phenomena, such as play, symbolism, and art, which are experienced as taking place in a kind of transitional space. These phenomena and this space are, and continue to be, essential to our ability to recover from the stress of living, to retreat from the outer world but remain connected to it; to have access to our inner world without becoming lost there. Making and enjoying art presumably require a successful experience with transitional objects and phenomena. The person whose early development goes awry here will be impoverished in her ability to enjoy what play potentially expands into, including, according to Winnicott, religious feeling, affection, dreaming, and the ability to enjoy and to make art.

I have considered tasks and vulnerabilities of the first year or so of life and how these nurture, motivate, or impinge on creative work later on. It bears repeating that work which accrues meaning or richness from this early phase may do so in ways that confer great pleasure. There is pleasure inherent in the sense of "oceanic oneness," in rhythm and repetition of sounds and sound patterns, in the sense of wholeness, of discovery, of being soothed, held and rocked. There is pleasure in the sense of words as magical, in their evocative power, in playfulness, in an appreciation of visual patterns, color, movement, and unity, in discovering the world as if for the first time. The capacity to enjoy such sensory and aesthetic experiences, and especially to create them, depends, at least in part, on our being able to revisit the aspects of early experience I've discussed here, without significant anxiety.

Experiences from the second and third years (see Settlage, 1989), contribute also to the joys and perils of creative work. The infant, then toddler, has a growing awareness that she is a separate being. This can be frightening. She senses her dependency, her great need for closeness and love, but she also has aggressive feelings, engendered in part by the threat of loss due to physical and emotional separations, and she fears that her aggression could threaten those vital relationships. The oscillations, for some, the struggles, which persist throughout life, between dependency and autonomy, intimacy and the sense of a separate self, are central to this stage. Where the outcome is mainly successful, the child will have a beginning ability to balance these opposing sets of needs, including in ways which support creativity. If the child's growing awareness and expression of separateness are felt actually to threaten essential relationships, however, as they did for the toddler whose mother recoiled when he attended to anyone or anything but her (chapter 5), then those aspects of other people or of creative work which later confront the child with her separateness, will make her greatly anxious, and so be feared.

The toddler is intrigued with her body and its products. She experiences her feces as her first creation, her first offering to the world, though she may also experience them as evidence of badness, messiness, as weapons or aggressive attacks because of fantasies of so using them or because of discomfort which may be associated with their production. As McDougall (1995) notes, "this unconscious libidinal origin [of making things] plays a vital role for the creative person in every domain [and is an] . . . important determinant of the capacity or incapacity to continue producing" (p. 59).

The toddler is interested in "anal messes" and enjoys playing with clay, mud, water, and finger paints. Such pleasures, unless discouraged or made to feel shameful, can have positive implications for creativity later on. They contribute to the likelihood the child will grow up to be playful and productive, to enjoy making things, and taking pride in what she makes. If the outcome of this stage is less fortunate, the child will instead come to feel embarrassed, self-conscious, or ashamed, to view her creations, including later artistic ones, as "shit," and herself as bad for attempting them. She may find it difficult to experiment with ideas, to generate new work, and may so need to make those ideas or that work conform to rigid notions of order or control that she kills what is promising in them, or turns from them in disgust or shame. Or, she may consider her every offering *too* precious to be questioned or modified. Such reactions point to the unconscious anal meanings that creativity and our creations can have for us, meanings which may be erotic, aggressive, or sadistic, and come from that time in early childhood when our productions were, in our imaginations at least, precious offerings, attacks on others, attempts to soil, to present a gift, or to control. Resistance to creative work based on the work's content (chapter 1) is often associated with this stage and with these meanings to us of our work.

During this stage, with her musculature, sphincter control, and sense of a separate self developing, the toddler begins to claim ownership of her body, some right to control its processes and products. She glories in the words *no* and *mine*. As she begins to assert her autonomy, her family is increasingly expecting her to conform to their standards of control and cleanliness. Some conflict inevitably ensues; the conflict leads to limit setting and frustration, which almost as inevitably evokes aggressive feelings in the child, followed by anxiety about that aggression.

Art cannot exist without aggression. Creative work involves and requires it (Segal, 1991, p. 92). Picasso reportedly said that each painting is an attack on reality; Galway Kinnell (1982, p. 92) has, in a poem, described the act of writing as an encounter with a bear whose identity and fierceness the poet must take on. Jane Hirshfield (1995) has observed how frequently the poetic act is compared by poets to being eaten by a lion. How is one to *attack* reality, *deface* the empty page or canvas, *twist* the metal, *cut* into stone, *break* with tradition or *break* new ground, if to do so feels too dangerous, aggressive, or forbidden? Yet this may be the result if during these early stages of development, the child comes to feel that aggression, even thoughts of it, endanger important relationships and threaten her with loss of love.

One who negotiates this developmental stage and its challenges well will have an easier time with self-regulation, be better able to exert control in appropriate, flexible ways, have access to, and be able to modulate, aggression. Where things go less well, she may be out of control, fear loss of control, struggle to control others, or exercise rigid self-control. Such control may cost her not only important access to healthy aggression, but also her spontaneity, playfulness, curiosity, creativity, and ability to learn.

A scientific researcher I saw in therapy lamented not being more creative and successful in his work. He was intellectually gifted, but feared giving up control, including over his own thoughts, and so had a hard time playing with possibilities and ideas. When he tried to problem solve, he'd choose an approach and stick with it even if it became clear the approach was leading nowhere. He was too frightened of making a mistake, "a mess," and looking stupid to be able to move on, to be freely curious. He saw that colleagues could be intuitive and creative, take risks, make errors, and "mess things up" without seeming to despair. He couldn't do this, but needed to work in familiar, predictable ways, and so tended to be plodding. He had difficulty tolerating ambiguity, and initially found therapy, the ambiguous venture we were embarked on, with its invitation to explore and discover, unsettling.

He knew how some of the great discoveries in science have occurred—the dream image which revealed the structure of the carbon molecule, Einstein's walk on the beach whereupon the answer to one of the questions about relativity that had been troubling him suddenly presented itself. My patient so feared losing control, however, presumably over his impulses and wishes, and especially his aggressive, even sadistic, ambitious ones, that he couldn't tolerate visiting those less rational, more intuitive parts of the mind that scientists and artists often rely on. He also had conflicts having to do with later developmental stages, specifically about competing with his father and being sexually assertive with women. These, too, made it difficult for him to be as effective as he would have liked. But it was the earlier concerns about control, messiness, and aggression, which were first apparent, because he reverted to these to protect himself from the dangers posed by his competitive and sexual strivings.

Over time, the experience of trying to say what occurred to him in therapy, and our work on why he so feared making mistakes, being assertive, ambitious, and curious, enabled him occasionally to surprise himself with associations and discoveries. He began to be able slightly to ease the control he had imposed on his inner life, to allow himself access to other levels of his knowledge and experience, other ways of using his skills. He began sometimes to solve problems more effectively and creatively—to play a little, to "mess around," to be less "orderly." He began also to be less frightened of his ambition and better able to assert himself.

He had no stated aspirations to be an artist. He did, however, want to be freer to innovate in his work, and began to see that his need for control and predictability were inimical to this, as they would be to any creative endeavor. He'd been stuck in fantasies, modes of operating which had their origins in the early years under consideration. He had feared losing control, autonomy, bodily products or parts, and love, that aggressive wishes would lead to catastrophe, that thoughts and wishes were dangerous. He felt he had to be extremely careful or he would reveal something messy and bad inside. All this had interfered with innovative thinking, making intuitive leaps, and drawing on his own unconscious sources.

The second and third years, in which such difficulties in part originate, are often also a time of excitement and pleasure—in bodily movement, sensorimotor skills, curiosity, including about anatomical differences, and in bodily display. Unless made to feel ashamed of wanting to do so, small children will enjoy showing themselves off and being admired, looking curiously at others, exploring sexual parts and differences. Their early experiences, including being looked at and looking, can contribute later to pleasure in the making of art, in showing what they have made, and admiring the productions of others.

If they end up instead feeling ashamed of, or guilty about, such pleasures and wishes, because of how they were responded to, or because of fantasies about these aspects of their inner lives, then their ability to create and to enjoy the creations of others will be limited. If, for example, they become conflicted about wishes to look or be looked at, they may grow up with curiosity inhibited—a hinderance to creative and most other pursuits. They may have difficulty performing, making things, or displaying them for the admiration and enjoyment of others. Such problems can have limited impact, as with a writer who becomes extremely anxious about reading in public, because to do so has problematical unconscious meanings for him, but is nonetheless able to write, publish, and even, despite the anxiety, to read. Or they can be quite damaging, as with a performance artist for whom performing unconsciously stood for masturbating in public (McDougall, 1995, p. 62), making him too anxious and ashamed to proceed.

I worked with one woman who was unable, until years into a lengthy therapy, even to hint at her long-cherished desires to write, sculpt, or paint. She couldn't reveal them to me or her feeling that she had talent in these areas, until we had worked at length on her several inhibitions, including a pronounced one about calling attention to, or displaying, herself. As a girl, she'd loved to perform in plays, have her body looked at appreciatively when she played sports, and be admired as a star student. She could enjoy these activities because they were expected of her by people she wanted to please, or were communal—shared by, or in the service of others. As a woman, she could hardly bring herself to appear in a bathing suit, wear makeup, or otherwise call attention to herself, especially to her body, though she knew she was fit and attractive. When she tried to do any of these things, she became quite anxious.

She had lost both parents as a small child and had had severe acne as an adolescent. Our work revealed that she had imagined these to be deserved punishments for many of her wishes, including some presumably from the developmental stage under consideration here, to exhibit herself to her parents, and particularly to her father, exciting his admiration and love. If these wishes had such horrible consequences, she seemed to have reasoned unconsciously early on, she would wish them no more. Nor, later in her development, did she allow herself other wishes having to do with competition and achievement. She had thus limited what she could have in her life and in this way tried to expiate her guilt and prevent further disaster. She had, at least for the first many years of the therapy, no idea that such bargains underlay her keeping herself from many longed-for pursuits and pleasures. She was so defended against her own wishes that most were strangers to her. The creative ones weren't; she knew of them, but instead of pursuing them, she had lived in the shadow of other people's accomplishments, longing to emerge, as years of therapy permitted her to begin gradually to do.

This woman's early losses, and especially her fantasies that the losses were her deserved punishment for her wishes, had made having such wishes, including to make art, seem dangerous. Less catastrophic experiences than hers, even fantasies themselves, can do the job. What we *imagine* it means or will lead to for us to see, be seen, or admired, can interfere with our ability to *show* ourselves or our work. Such difficulties may be slight or severe, specific or general.

The meanings to us of creative work, our pleasures in and motivations for doing it, as well as the obstacles to it that we encounter, can have origins in later developmental levels or stages. One of these, the oedipal phase, from approximately the middle of the third through the fifth year of life, I will consider in detail. I will then touch briefly on stages subsequent to this one.

During the oedipal phase, when the girl falls in love with her father and the boy with his mother, the child feels possessive, desirous, competitive, and fearful of punishment, or retaliation. Themes now emerge which have influenced millenia of history, mythology, and the arts: sexual rivalry (the eternal triangle), incest and incestuous wishes, jealousy and betrayal, competitiveness, ambition, regicide, patricide, matricide, infanticide, guilt and punishment, or expiation, renunciation, battles among desire, fear, and conscience. The child's success in accomplishing the difficult tasks of this stage will have profound implications for the future, including for his or her ability to do creative work.

The child who negotiates this stage well, and I will explain what I mean by this shortly, will be more likely later to see herself as having a legitimate claim to her chosen work, a right to compete, and if possible to succeed. She will be unlikely to suffer guilt over legitimate aspirations, including creative (and procreative) ones. If she negotiates this stage less successfully, she may have difficulty competing because to do so may stand for competing with and potentially surpassing parents or authority figures, who she fears she may harm, be punished by, or kill off. Competing may unconsciously stand for competing with one parent for the other and so feel dangerous or forbidden. If interested in creative work, one who has such unconscious conflicts about competing or striving may encounter significant anxiety or resistance. The creative process itself may unconsciously represent to her the forbidden competition. The creative product may stand for proof of an incestuous union. She may fear punishment for the aggression that creative work requires, and the excitement it involves, and so hold herself back from it, or pay for it with creative blocks, guilt, or depression.

A person with significant unresolved difficulties from this stage may, regardless of age and circumstance, unconsciously consider herself not to be an adult with the accompanying right to strive for competence, to compete, be sexual, procreate, and create. She may fear that to claim the powers of the adult will lead to terrible punishment. Such was the fate of Prometheus, who stole fire from the gods to give it to mere men, and was punished by daily having his liver torn out, only to have it grow back and be torn out again. Eve obtained knowledge that was supposed to be God's alone and she and Adam were banished from God's garden. She thenceforth would have labor pains (and, no doubt, PMS and menopause as well). She was punished by having the bringing forth of a new creation, which could stand for a baby or a work of art, be an arduous, if not risky, endeavor. That the treasures which Prometheus and Eve appropriated, fire and knowledge, are associated with sexuality, that such appropriation is punished by angry gods, and with physical suffering, is relevant here. Certainly the 3- or 4-year-old who wants to deprive powerful adults of what is both precious and theirs, expects them to be angry and to punish accordingly. That the punishments of Prometheus and Eve involve being banished by angry fathers—thrown off Mt. Olympus or out of Eden—and made by them to suffer physically, should be no surprise, especially to the psychoanalytically informed. The nature of the suffering—having an organ ripped out (or off) repeatedly by large, angry birds, fearing bodily harm as the price for having a baby—seems consistent with what a small child might expect as punishment for competitive and sexual strivings.

I worked briefly with a rare book dealer who came to see me because of an unresolved love triangle involving himself, his somewhat older wife, whom he had desired until she began to want a child with him, and a younger woman, unable to have children. He felt hopelessly torn between the two and could commit himself to neither. Nor, it turned out, could he commit himself to me or the therapy, which eventually led us to stop. With me, too, he imposed limits on the relationship which prevented its reaching fruition.

It became apparent that when his wife wanted him to father her child, to assume an adult role, which I believe he felt was forbidden him, she became for him a maternal figure toward whom his previous feelings of desire seemed, mysteriously, to vanish. He began then to direct his sexual interest elsewhere. He felt devoted to his wife, dependent on her, and guilty for wanting to leave her for a life "away from home" with the younger woman. He saw his wife as good, kind, but no longer desirable. To imagine their having a child together was somehow impossible. Yet to leave her for the younger woman felt like a cruel, hurtful abandonment, as if he were wanting to leave home and an old mother who needed and had been good to him.

At one point, he mentioned casually that he had longed to be a musician and had studied to be one. He had taken up the same instrument that his father, also a musician, still played in our local symphony orchestra. On one occasion, shortly before his father had an important concert, the son had borrowed his father's instrument—it was one of the larger ones and not easily misplaced—and managed inadvertently to "lose" it. His guilt over losing his *father's instrument* had nearly paralyzed him. He'd found himself unable, after that, to play music. He had given it up entirely, inexplicably, and with great sadness, but also with what I found to be a noteworthy lack of curiosity about why he had done so.

He was unable to think about the determinants of that decision, or of his having borrowed and lost what stood for his father's power and creativity, as having been in any way significant. Though bright, and familiar with psychoanalytic concepts, he could think of the matter only in the most concrete terms. He couldn't attach any meanings to his having essentially stolen from his father that which stood for the father's power and was the means whereby the father made his living. Neither could he attach any meanings to his guiltily feeling that he must (presumably to expiate the crime) relinquish any related power of his own, including his own music and now the power to father a child. He couldn't allow himself to discover that within the symbolic crime and chosen punishment were revealed both his oedipal wish to defeat his father, to appropriate what was his father's—penis, power, ability to create—and his self-imposed punishment for those wishes. He could allow himself neither to make music nor to make babies. He couldn't be a husband to the wife who, when she wanted a child, suddenly seemed to represent the forbidden, renounced maternal figure, or leave her to start a new life. Nor could he stay in therapy and create something with me. He could not, at least at that time or with me, unearth the meanings of his paralysis in the love triangle and get freed up to assume the role of a creative and perhaps also procreative adult. I, too, became a woman to whom he couldn't commit and with whom he couldn't create something.

Loewald (1980a), in "The Waning of the Oedipus Complex," says that if we do not, *in our inner world,* kill off our parents psychologically, and appropriate their power, their authority over us, we do not grow up. In his words, "without the guilty deed of parricide, there is no autonomous self" (p. 393). He says that not only must we kill them off internally; we must bear our guilty feelings for having done so and for the incestuous fantasies and wishes which accompany this stage. People who do not accomplish these requisite psychological acts in the eventual assuming of adulthood, who fail to make the internal break with their parents as sources of ultimate power and authority, and so to assume power and authority in their own right, will be limited in their abilities to develop and use their talents, or compete. "Parents" in this context may, as Harold Bloom (1973) has noted, include progenitors in the creative sphere, the famous predecessor poet, writer, or artist who casts a giant shadow.

To create requires an ability to identify with both parents' sexual functions (McDougall, 1991, pp. 559–581). We must be able both to fertilize, or engender the work, and to gestate and give birth to it. Impaired identifications with the gender or the sexual function of either parent, will get in the way of the parthenogenesis creativity entails. This is also true of failing to resolve guilt over loving and identifying with both parents and desiring both, as small children do, and over the natural, but often unconscious wish to be both sexes and experience the procreative functionings of both.

Such feelings of prohibition and guilt come, of course, from that most significant legacy of this phase, the superego (see also chapter 7). Its development is crucial. The small child, to preserve his or her relationship with both parents and be spared punishment for sexual and aggressive wishes toward them, begins, as we know, to relinquish the (usually opposite-sex) parent as an object of desire and to identify with the (usually same-sex) parent instead. In this way, the child imagines that she will preserve her parents' love, and grow up to be like them, thus having both their approval and eventually their prequisites in the world. As she identifies with her parents (modifies her self-image or *self representation* until it resembles her view of them), the child gradually relinquishes some of her passionate ties to them and some of her utter reliance on them as figures of authority and power. As in mourning, when we identify with someone as part of the process of giving him or her up, but come to have something of the lost person within us, the child, in relinquishing the parents as objects of desire, sets aspects of them up internally as the superego.

Derived from the parental values, which if humane become the basis for the child's eventual morality and ethicality, the superego has the authority and power to guide our decisions and actions as the parents originally did, to make us feel validated and loved, or disapproved of and guilty. Its authority is often harsher, more irrational than the parents were, and may be quick to punish and severe about what it deems unacceptable, including the excitement, pleasure, and unconscious meanings involved in creative work. Such strictness may exist even where the parents were flexible and loving because the superego is based, at least initially, on the small child's view of justice, which tends to be primitive and harsh (incestuous wishes are feared to lead to castration, aggressive feelings to abandonment).

If this often strict and irrational internal agency doesn't get modified over time, it may condemn the child, later the adult, for wanting to do what may stand for forbidden excitement, "adult" pleasures, and transgressions of various sorts. And, unless the relationship of the child to the parent is impaired in ways that interfere with the development of the superego, it will have an arsenal with which to enforce its authority: the power, that is, to make us feel loved and valued, or guilty and worthless, including in relationship to the wish to do or the doing of creative work.

The stage known as latency, from 6 or 7 to the onset of adolescence, contributes also to the ability or inability to create. During latency, if things have gone well and continue to do so, much learning occurs, skills develop, and interests which may prove lifelong begin to be explored. The child develops the capacity to use "signal anxiety," a kind of low dose alarm signal which may not even register consciously but leads to the instituting of defensive strategies in response to what are felt to be dangers from within. This development allows the child to *use* anxiety in the service of protecting herself rather than be flooded or overwhelmed by large doses of it and thus kept from learning or attending to other things. Developmental problems or failures here can leave the child prone to problems with anxiety and so interfere with learning, the development of discipline, and the ability to master information and skills, thus compromising creative and other work later on. Of course if this anxiety warning is set off in response to feelings, wishes, or actions which are essential to creative work, such as curiosity or excitement, anxiety will be a problem for creativity, though of a different sort than when it overwhelms.

Through the disappointments inevitable in any relationship, the child, if fortunate, gradually learns during these years to give up her idealized versions of her parents, to develop and tolerate a more realistic picture of them, and of herself. This makes it easier for her later to tolerate imperfection in others and in herself, to persist at things she may find difficult, including in the arts, without feeling ashamed or humiliated when she can't do them instantly or perfectly.

Too abrupt, great, or early a disillusionment with her parents, or herself and her own limited powers and skills, will interfere with this developmental task, with problematical implications for creative work. For how is one to do such work if seeing its flaws, or one's own, is intolerable?

During latency, curiosity normally begins greatly to expand the child's world. Conscious fantasy and daydream can flourish, the imagination becomes a source of great pleasure and solace, giving the child the means to play out dramas, try on roles, and experiment with interests and activities. The trying on of new roles and exploring of new interests may lead the child to discover some which prove enduring. Many writers, artists, musicians, dancers, actors, and others started making up stories, writing poems, drawing, playing an instrument, dancing, or performing during these years (see chapter 9). If anxiety doesn't function as a signal, however, but floods the child instead, or if too much from the previous stages is unresolved, the child will have difficulty making optimal use of these important years to learn, experiment, and discover what he or she is good at and loves.

Adolescence contributes too, far more than my brief consideration of it will suggest. An important task of the adolescent stage is to resume, recapitulate, and carry forward that process the oedipal child in part left off. This includes the further relinquishing, even mourning, of her intimate childhood relationship with her parents, so she can move into a more independent though connected life. It includes further renouncing the incestuous wishes toward the parents and becoming her own person, now at the more advanced developmental level, and establishing her identity as an individual with the body, desires, and procreative capacities of an adult. Conflicts about sexuality, about whether one has the right to adult-level sexual and other functioning, may express themselves in feeling one hasn't the right to create, to be excited and alive about one's creative potential, and fully to realize it.

Success in adolescent development allows eventually for the establishing of a sense of individual, adult identity, of independent thought and action, including in the moral sphere, not just defiance of or submission to family or social values, or the values of a group. The person who doesn't succeed here will be less able to think for herself, to create work which expresses her individuality. She may need instead to destroy, or to create only what defies or defers to tradition, whether or not it has inherent worth and expresses who she is and what she believes or feels.

Each of the developmental stages, then, potentially contributes to the capacity or incapacity to enjoy and to do creative work. Each potentially contributes to art's themes, to the psychological richness, the resonance and power we experience in creating and enjoying art. Each can contribute to the sense of depth and recognition art evokes in us, to the nuances which enrich and deepen it, to the basic human conflicts it can embody and address. At the same time, each stage presents potential pitfalls and challenges to our eventual capacity to do such work. Even if we've traversed the developmental stages with relative success, each leaves us with potential vulnerabilities, anxieties, and conflicts with which the creative work of others may help us and to which our own creative work may help enable us to speak.

7

HELP AND HINDERANCE FROM THE INNER WORLD

In a letter, a friend wrote:

> For the first time, (I) went on the attack with the voice that tends to get
> after me about how terrible my work is. Usually . . . I write out dialogues
> when I'm feeling blocked . . . the horrible belittling things the voice is
> saying to me, and my defensive responses, and . . . that usually enables
> me to work again because I realize how mean this voice is (Voice: what-
> ever made you think you could write? Me: I like to write. Voice:. . . that
> doesn't mean you have any aptitude for it! and on for several pages).
> This time I . . . was just as mean to the critical voice as it has been to
> me, which turned out to be energizing . . . even fun. . . . I seem to have
> driven it into a corner, and . . . have been able to work pretty well.
> (Sterling, 1997, personal communication)

Her strategy reminds me of a notice I saw in a National Park Forest
on what to do if you encounter a cougar: Don't run. Stand your
ground. Draw yourself up to look as tall as possible. Spread your
arms and plant your feet to look as broad and formidable as possible.
Speak in an authoritative voice. Stand there, that is, looking brave,
and order the beast to Go Away.

Gail Godwin (1995) describes her version of the voice as a
Watcher at the Gate, a term she borrows from Schiller as quoted by
Freud. The Watcher is critical of and would censor that flow of
thoughts and images out of which art may grow. Godwin decided,
in self-defense, to make her Watcher's acquaintance. She drew his
portrait, gave him a name, engaged in dialogues with him. She described him—character, appearance, and attire—in hilarious detail.
He became her "daily regular." She grew fond of and learned to
coexist with him, and so diminished his power. It seems the voice or
Watcher must be coaxed or ordered from his controlling position
at the gate, driven into a corner, or somehow befriended, if we are
to have access to those places in us where art begins.

Artists and writers I see in therapy often describe the voice as if it were uniquely their affliction, as perhaps they believe it to be. Some take it as proof they lack talent or aren't meant to make art. They fight it, or succumb, depending on what in them and their lives speaks on their behalf or on behalf of their work. A man who loves to paint and is apparently talented, but rarely allows himself this pleasure, finds that when a painting is nearly finished, he is barraged by thoughts like these: "How *dare* you think you can paint. Look how *bad* this is! Compare it with ... " The names of great artists he especially admires follow in rapid, humiliating succession. A fiction writer, when she tries to write, often has a voice in her head which recounts her various rejections by editors, then enumerates her friends' successes, as if she'd had no successes of her own and her friends didn't frequently get work rejected as well. This alleged disparity she takes as proof that she, unlike others, has neither the talent nor the right.

I've had a long personal acquaintance with the Watcher, or voice. Lately I find that it speaks when my writing begins to take off. Something interesting happens; the language goes some place new; the voice hisses, in tones worthy of Iago, "Do you really want to say *that*? Trite, isn't it? Sentimental?" That the voice speaks as I begin to write something promising angers me. Increasingly I tell it to shut up. I tell it that I don't know, and won't, until after I finish writing and revising, so I will write now and evaluate later. I try to shrug off or shout down its mean, premature opinion, to deny its right to intervene.

Probably every artist is acquainted with the Watcher. The poets I interviewed (chapter 9), each of whom has produced good books, and several of whom have won honors and prizes, nonetheless all know it well. Writers and artists who persist seem to be those who find ways to coexist with, or to defeat the voice. They manage, as one interviewee put it, "to make friends with despair." Do the ones who keep going simply have more talent? I suspect that among those who give up, or struggle but can't achieve what they seem to have the potential for, some also have the talent, but find the voice so daunting and hear so little from within to oppose it that it eventually beats them down.

I hope it's clear that by "voice," I mean thoughts which may seem *as if* they were voices in one's head, feelings we experience *as if* they were being uttered. I am not talking about hallucinations or delusions. I hope it's also clear that what often seems like a voice and will be referred to here as a voice, sometimes manifests itself instead as an inexplicable shift in mood, an attack of self-doubt or guilt, a wave of hope or despair, as if something had been whispered almost within earshot and were influencing us, although we aren't sure what, or by whom.

There are, in fact, several voices to consider in thinking about what helps and what hinders creativity. There is the voice of the story or poem trying to speak, a voice whose source is inexplicable, but with whom many are acquainted. Godwin, in the same essay, writes of the "angel" whose voice the writer listens for because it heralds the story or poem; we also know this as the muse. There is the sustaining voice, sometimes from within, sometimes borrowed from a friend, teacher, or parent. This voice says go on, you're good enough, you deserve to do this; besides, no one else can paint your pictures or write your poems. There is the voice that waits until we have a draft, a sense of what we're doing, then speaks critically but helpfully, offering reasonable, informed, constructive advice: This line falls flat, that image doesn't fit here, this is good, keep going. While not always an accurate judge, it is well meaning, often judicious, and serves the process well. For some, there is a voice which praises profusely, even aggrandizes—how great, utterly great, you're a genius. This one becomes problematical if it mindlessly persists, not allowing a cooler appraisal, and revision. Most, perhaps all, writers and artists also know the attacking, guilt-bearing voice that says your work is worthless, you lack talent, you're presumptuous to be trying. And there is the voice, perhaps this one is really the same as the previous voice, though there may be two or more of them, that questions the worth of a thought, line, or image, doubts our abilities, our rights, as if intent on defeating us. This last may be Godwin's Watcher at the Gate, my friend's mean-spirited, though momentarily cornered, pest. These are the voices that sustain or attack us. Even those of us who are psychoanalytically informed, practitioners or veterans of therapy or analysis, sometimes wonder: What *are* they? *Where* do they come from?

As therapists, we think of them as thoughts, feelings, self-doubts, with origins in various components of the psyche, components I will discuss below. As writers, artists, we know them as muses, or saboteurs. To think about their nature and origins usefully, we do well, clinicians and artists both, to consider psychological development. Specifically we need to remember the developmental process whereby aspects of the external world get established within. I refer to *internalization*, through which each of us first creates for him- or herself a representational world (Sandler and Rosenblatt, 1962).

People and things become "represented" in the mind by enduring images of them so we can remember, think, imagine, and plan. Sandler and Rosenblatt (1962) note that such *representations* are made up of many different images experienced over time. They are more stable and enduring than images, though they may change their shape from moment to moment, showing us different facets, and causing those often mysterious subtle shifts in our feelings toward others and ourselves. Important people in our lives become set up within us as object representations or internal objects, our relationships with them as internal object relations. These representations permit us, if all goes well, to stay emotionally connected with people who are important to us, despite anger and disappointments, separations, and change. We also become represented for ourselves internally; we develop a self representation which, like our object representations, is built up of many images, and, if all goes well, similarly enables us to experience ourselves as whole, coherent, and consistent, despite ranges in feelings, fluctuations in self-esteem, changes in health or circumstance.

Once those by whom we were originally guided are represented within, those whose love and approval we sought and needed, and continue to seek and need, usually parents and later teachers, we transfer to the images we have internalized, some of the authority and status that belonged originally to the actual people. They thus become a special kind of object representation, an introject, and have the power to make us behave and feel like a child in the presence of a parent. The establishing of the representational world, and especially of introjects, is part of the building of psychic structure whereby what in the outer world previously guided and protected us comes now to do so from within.

The most influential introject is the superego (see chapter 6), with its power to make us feel approved or disapproved of, guilty or ashamed. Also important for how we feel about and conduct ourselves is the ego ideal. An aspect of the superego, the ego ideal is a representation of those ideals, attainable or unattainable, that we hold up for ourselves and against which we measure who and what we are. How we feel about ourselves, whether our allotment of self-esteem is large or small, steady or constantly fluctuating, depends in part on the nature of the ego ideal and how well or poorly we measure up.

These now internal agencies or structures, imbued with the power, authority, and values the parents or parent figures originally had, help us regulate our behavior, establish our goals, determine and compare ourselves with the ideals we strive toward, maintain our self-esteem, shape what we allow ourselves to think, want, and do. They determine moment to moment, and through the course of our lives, how we see and feel about ourselves. They enable us, therefore, to become independent of others while taking on some of their values and standards and those of the culture.

Once we have set up this inner world through the process of internalization, we live in that world no less, and usually more, than in the external one. The internal world functions also as a lens through which, often unknowingly, we view, interact with, and interpret the external one, and see ourselves. Our internalizations, along with learning and the ways we come, characteristically, to resolve internal conflicts—the defenses we use, the impulses and wishes we permit ourselves—contribute to the building of further psychic structure. Over time, for better or for worse, this structure increasingly takes the place of external guidance and control, regulation, reward and punishment, motivation, and comforting. Any aspect of this representational world and of psychic structure may greatly support our creativity or impede it. Certainly, our internal objects influence creative work and are among the several sources of these sustaining, or reproaching, voices and Watchers at the Gate.

Pines (1993, pp. 103–114) describes a woman in analysis who couldn't write because of what she did unconsciously with her own destructive wishes. She felt "fused" with her (internal object) mother and experienced her own destructiveness as if it were her mother's, now directed at her.

Fearing an attack from within, in the form, no doubt, of depression, guilt, or persecutory feelings, she projected this destructiveness of hers next onto the outside world, then feared that readers would be hostile and attacking. Later, presumably through analysis, she became able to write if she imagined writing for her dead father who, because of her positive memory of him, was receptive and encouraging. She could write because of this good internal object who encouraged her and perhaps protected her from the bad one. We see how both the prohibiting, attacking (here, maternal) and the encouraging (here, paternal) voices, or objects, though not consciously "heard" and available for dialogue like Godwin's, are present and help to determine whether the person they inhabit feels permitted to create.

McDougall (1995, p. 100) writes about her analytic work with a blocked writer who, like Pines' patient, projected onto her (internal) mother her own destructive tendencies, though the history suggests that the actual mother had indeed been destructive. This, presumably, made the patient feel rid of her own dangerous aggressiveness, but now under threat from her mother within. Her next defensive strategy, too, was to "reproject" the aggression onto an imagined audience, for whom it then became impossible to write. McDougall notes that this blocked writer thereby managed to experience herself as having no responsibility for the resulting attack on her own creativity. She also suggests (1995, pp. 58–59) that an artist's or writer's public is composed of the *internal* public, which may be hostile or supportive, that what is projected onto the external audience from the inner world is decisive for what the artist can achieve.

We can project what we hesitate to own not only onto internal objects, or external readers, editors, critics, and reviewers, but onto *the work itself,* causing it to seem bad or dangerous, and so to be held in check, turned away from, or destroyed. Bergmann (1997) suggests this, too. She notes that the aggressive feelings we originally had toward important others, but felt we had to protect them from in order to preserve our relationship to them, may "get displaced or projected (onto what we make), leading to work paralysis or destruction of the product" (p. 203).

What we can project onto readers, or displace onto our creations, we can also turn directly against ourselves. Those internal mothers, fathers, teachers, formed out of our experiences with them, but also often distorted by our wishes, desires, guilts, and fears, may take up residence as the attacking or sustaining voices in our head. They, and the feelings we have for them, and perceive ourselves as receiving from them, may be what attacks us ("Who said you could write? That poem is dreck! Everything you write is dreck"), or encourages ("You can do it!"), enabling us to go on. They may offer both. Their stance may depend on what a given work represents to us, on what we imagine it does or would to them, on whatever wishes, impulses, longings, fantasies are ascendant, on how we feel about the favorable or unfavorable reactions of others to our work.

Our internal objects are essential to us and to our creativity. If we experience them as receptive, encouraging, they may help us to keep going. We may create as an offering to them—a short story was one author's valentine for his mother. We may become blocked to prevent ourselves from attacking them, if our art represents or feels to us like an attack. We may hesitate to do creative work if we imagine that work will provoke them to attack, hate, or abandon us. We may become blocked to withhold from them if the creation feels like a coerced or dangerous offering of love, something their narcissism requires of us, or if we feel they hate us. We may be unable or refuse to create as an expression of a struggle with them over who shall possess that which we or our bodies produce, or out of guilt that makes us feel we don't deserve their approval or their love.

We may write to repair damage we feel we have done to them by being separate, or through other expressions of aggression, or not write to demonstrate damage we feel they have done to us. We may be blocked because we feel estranged from, unable to trust or to feel loved by them, or because we feel seen by them as barren or unworthy. Our silence may be a reproach, as one blocked painter's was a reproach to his depressed, withholding mother. We may write to make them love us, or not write to make them love us—or both, as was the case for a novelist whose mother needed her daughter's success in order to feel good about herself, then envied and sought to appropriate it. We may be like the poet who, as a small child, composed poems at bedtime and, too young to write them down, called her mother in to write them down for her. The poems delayed their goodnight, wooed the mother, and forestalled sleep. This poet apparently has insomnia and hates to be alone at night; perhaps when she is, she senses something unsettling in her relationship with an internal object, a relationship in which her art has played a helpful and important role.

It has been suggested that the rituals many writers go through before they begin, sharpening a dozen number 2 pencils, arranging cherished objects on the desk, serve not only to help manage the anxiety that sitting down to work mobilizes, but to invoke the muse. In the present context, it should be clear what or who the muse represents, why we need to summon, placate, or cajole her. Certainly she can be thought of as an expression of an internal object, with the power to inspire creative work, or to keep that work becalmed.

Such internal objects, then, influence our creativity in many ways. They can nurture, sustain, berate, persecute, or threaten to abandon us; they may do several of these. Some may threaten, others sustain; some nurture, as long as they approve of what we are doing, but abandon or attack if we venture into emotional territories they don't admire or condone.

Milner (1957) has said much that is salient here, including this:

> [T]he substance of experience is what we bring to what we see, without our own contribution, we see nothing. But . . . imagination itself does not spring from nothing, it is what we have made within us out of all past relationships with what is outside, whether they were realized as outside relationships or not. (pp. 26–28)

The self representation is another source of those voices that help or hinder creative work. A counterpart to the object representation, the self representation is made up of our experiences over time including how others respond to us and reflect us back. It includes our sense of that mixture of abilities and vulnerabilities we have been dealt, or find our way to, how we see ourselves, and what we believe we are permitted in our lives. Our self representation may be such that we think, "Yes, I'm a poet, I'm talented, and I have the right to be a poet." Or, "No, this is for others; for me, this isn't possible or allowed."

The introject also has great relevance for creativity, and especially for the question of permission or prohibition. (It has relevance for the horror film genre as well, in which victims are taken over by alien or supernatural beings who inhabit the victims' bodies or brains and then rule them from within.) In other instances of internalization, identification, for example, the child comes to behave or think as the parent does. Where there is an introject, the child, and later perhaps also the adult, behaves *as if* the parent were present. He or she does so because the introject is invested with the parent's authority and comes into being, paradoxically, as part of the process which potentially makes us independent of that authority. The presence of an introject can be inferred, for example, when a young child who is not supposed to eat cookies before meals hesitates to take one, though no one is present to witness the possible transgression, and the cookie beckons loudly. The cookie may ultimately win over the introject, but if it does, the child will feel uneasy, even guilty or ashamed, and may confess the offense or find a way to be punished for it. Consider the cookie now as standing for other pleasures which feel prohibited, including making art.

If an introject prohibits pleasure, excitement, aggression, self-absorption, it will object to activities, including creative ones, which involve these and may do so aggressively. No doubt introjects account for some of the more vociferous voices of prohibition which writers and other artists know so well. Introjects are generally dealt with by submission (we obey them), or by identification (we modify the self representation so it is more like the introject and presumably more acceptable to it) (Sandler & Rosenblatt, 1962). Introjects can therefore present a problem for creative work. Where they oppose such work or oppose the feelings, fantasies, and wishes which accompany it, they may indeed need to be driven into corners, or brought to the therapist's office or the analyst's couch.

Introjects are, in the nonpsychotic at least, supposed to be, and to remain, unconscious. They are supposed to manifest themselves subtly, making us uneasy, anxious, or guilty, or causing us suddenly to feel the need to be doing something other than what we set out to do. But I propose that they also manifest themselves more directly and consciously in the form of those opposing, malevolent voices or presences which many have described.

To illustrate how this may work, I present an introject of my own with whom I am quite consciously acquainted. She is Madame K, my internal representation (turned introject) of my high school French teacher. When her students didn't pay sufficient attention in class, Mme. K would slam her ruler down on the desk in front of the adolescent dreamer, to startling effect. Mme. K also had a slightly pained expression in response to even minor mispronunciations of the language she loved. She was determined to teach us to avoid these.

During the decades since I last saw her, Mme. K has made her presence known to me whenever, after a long hiatus, I have attempted to speak French. I mispronounce, or hesitate over the proper inflection, and Madame's face appears before me, saddened by what I have done or am about to do. On occasion, her ruler thwacks an imagined desk, startling me. I have never had a teacher, not even one who taught a course that was more personally signifi- cant for me, or who had a more troubling pedagogic style, so live on in my head, her authority and power intact. I *have* had former clinical supervisors suddenly float over an hour, happily unseen by the patient, and tactfully assist, kindly praise, or gently chide me. And I've had invisible writing teachers suddenly speak in my ear in encouraging (ah!) or cautioning (oops!) tones. These, however, have felt more like fond memories, the evoking of comforting or helpful presences—more like benevolent object representa- tions—than like the abrupt, uninvited appearance on the scene of something with residual power over me and imposed opinions of its own. My fondly remembered supervisors and teachers haven't had, or made use of, the force of the nonetheless fondly remembered Mme. K. *She* insists on correct pronunciation. She has, more than once, caused me to falter before a waiter or a Metro clerk until I could summon the precise inflection of which she would approve.

She has, I trust, no bearing on my writing. Nor to my knowledge does she stand for anyone else who has been significant for me. Yet her presence when I attempt to speak French, *and only then*, carries with it all her power over my 15-year-old self, and I think of her when I try to consider or to explain to students the nature of an introject. While grateful for the French she taught me, I am more grateful she makes no appearance at my writing desk, though other denizens of my inner world no doubt do. I sympathize with those before whose computer or easel their own Mme. K appears, prohib- iting the essential trial and error, false starts, and mispronunciations that creative work requires.

An introject with far greater influence on our ability to do cre- ative work is the superego, that malevolent and/or benign internal agency which, as we know, stands for the authority of the parents, usually the father, and is, as Freud taught us, heir to and outcome of the Oedipus complex. The superego tells us when we're good or lovable, punishes us for thoughts, wishes, and actions it deems unworthy. The offending thought, wish, or action, actual or imag- ined, may be unconscious; so may the superego's response. We may not even know we are feeling guilty. We may instead suddenly be filled with self-critical thoughts, self-loathing, an inability to experi- ence pleasure, satisfaction, or hope.

I described a painter (chapter 2) for whom each advance in her work, and the therapy, was followed by an attack of guilt and depression, hallmarks of her superego and measures of its severity, as well as of how strong her unconscious wish was to defy it. After a period of success and the accompanying pleasure, she'd feel guilty, become depressed, be unable to work, and for months feel hopeless. Her confidence in her art, her excitement about any recognition or encouragement she'd received, would vanish from her awareness, or if she remembered them, they would have been rendered meaningless and could give her no pleasure.

These attacks by her superego, and various hostile internal objects, seemed to occur in response to a range of feelings and wishes she feared were unacceptable. Ambition had been prohibited for girls in her family. Competitive strivings were forbidden, especially when these were directed at a sib whom she'd already surpassed in many ways. Excitement elicited guilt, because it involved pleasure and because when she was feeling it, she was less concerned with the welfare of humanity and more focused on her own life and wishes. Unacceptable were her longings to go off on her own and enjoy herself rather than spend her life worrying about whether she was paying sufficient attention to me, her therapist/mother/father, whom she experienced at these times as existing to control her for my/our own invidious purposes.

It took careful analysis of all this over a period of years for her to begin to feel that it might be legitimate for her to have in her life that which excited her, opened worlds for her, and gave her the opportunity to make a place for herself as a person and an artist. For this woman, her superego, which attacked with guilt and reproach and made her feel worthless, was a primary source of the undermining voices I have described, though her internal objects often loudly joined the chorus.

My own experience has been that breakthroughs in my writing tend to be followed not by depression, but by its cousin, silence. I refer not to the fallow silence many require after a piece of work has been finished, but to a silence that feels self-punishing, as if I have transgressed in achieving whatever the new work does, in demonstrating that I can do something better now, or more bravely, than before. This doesn't manifest itself as a voice—no conscious Mme. K here—but as a sudden reticence about writing. I can, at such times, come up with endless justifications for not writing, usually having to do with obligations to others, which I can then come to resent, as if they, and not I, were putting up barriers between me and my work. This seems to be a way of expiating whatever I feel I must in order eventually to write again. While this is my particular version, such struggles characterize the course of many attempts to make art.

Segal's observation (Segal, 1991, p. 92) that "there can be no art without aggression" bears repeating here. McDougall (1995) has similarly noted that her clinical work with creative persons and reflections on it have led [her] to conclude that *violence is an essential element* in all creative productions" (p. 55). These statements can be understood not only if we consider the artist's seeming attack on her materials but also the tensions inherent in art, and, as Segal notes, the incomplete resolution of conflict that the art may represent. Where aggression is prohibited by that most powerful introject, the superego, it may be impossible to do creative work, or one may do it, like my artist patient and countless others, only at a price.

The superego may prohibit creative work or make us feel guilty for doing it because the work stands for forbidden rivalry with parents or siblings, threats to parental or other authority, or the fulfillment of incestuous or competitive wishes. The poem, book, or painting may unconsciously stand for the baby the artist wished, as a small child, to have with mother or father, and so be regarded as shameful or forbidden. Creative work, or the results of it, may stand for dangerous products or priceless treasures from the body, erotic pleasure experienced in bringing it into being, signs of one's separateness, or longings to abolish separateness and be as one. If the superego is harsh and rigid, as the small child once imagined the parents to be, rather than benign and flexible in its judgments and what it permits, it will object to the meanings to us of our materials or medium, our hopes or ambitions for our work, or (see chapter 2) to any of the unconscious meanings, or implications, the creative act or product may have for us. And if it *does* object, the superego can do so via those voices which so daunt us.

The superego may object to the kinds of knowing the art reveals, particularly if the art tends, as good art does, to be impolite, unconventional, nondeferential, questioning of authority or tradition, unsettling, acknowledging of what in us we are inclined in most contexts to deny, ignore, or conceal. The superego will object to the excitement and pleasure the creative act involves, if excitement and pleasure are what it prohibits. It will object, that is, if it judges the creative act to violate any of the exaggeratedly strict laws the small child ascribes to her parents at the age when the superego comes into being if, in the course of time and experience, its strictness hasn't been modified or eased.

A novelist read a small group of us a chapter based, I later learned, on her family's history. After reading us the chapter, she broke down. She said she felt ashamed, as if in reading us the work she "had vomited all over" us. That the work was artistically stunning, that it had been well received, seemed not to be the point. The work from which she had read had to do with her recent uncovering of secrets about her family's origins and cultural heritage. These were secrets which in wartime had been crucial to the family's survival, but they had, inexplicably and at psychological cost, been kept for decades after, even from the writer and her brothers. This secrecy, and her sensing of it, had clouded her childhood. She'd set out as an adult to learn the truth about herself and her family. Then, having done so, she'd felt impelled to write about it. When her family learned what she was doing, they accused her of being hostile to them, claiming (though there was no apparent reason to think this could be so) that if she published the material, she would destroy them. She felt torn about what to do and burdened with guilt.

This writer was self-aware and introspective enough to know that her motives were complex and might include the desire to punish those who had withheld the truth from her and in so doing, caused her difficulty. That she might have complex motives, that the family's claim she was trying to hurt them might in part be true, seemed to trouble her even more than their anger. She struggled with questions about whether she had the right to tell the story which was hers but belonged also to others.

It seemed to me that this writer's conflicts might also have been over having symbolically to kill off her parents and their authority in order to claim her own identity. In deciding to tell the story she had been ordered not even to know, though it was also her own, she was indeed taking on the task that Loewald (1980a) described. She was further establishing her autonomous self through an act which symbolically stood for killing off her parents and bearing the guilt for this crime. Not to do so would mean, in this area at least, not to become more fully her own person. To do so meant bearing the guilt.

The superego also contains the ego ideal, that internal representation of our highest ideals and expectations for ourselves. Whether our internalized ideals are flexible, realistic, and attainable, or perfectionistic and impossible to satisfy, the superego measures us against these and bases our allotment of self-esteem or self-love on how well we do here. The superego may respond to us like a loving, admiring parent who is occasionally disappointed in, but basically loves and values us. Or it may respond like a parent we can never please or satisfy, who continually makes us feel we just aren't good enough, refusing to take into account our intentions, give us credit for trying, or recognize the legitimate need for time and practice, trial and error. How tolerant the superego is of us and how attainable are the ideals will not necessarily directly reflect how we were brought up. What is internalized is shaped or distorted en route by our perceptions, fantasies, and feelings, and can therefore be much tougher or stricter than were our actual parents.

That all this has direct relevance for creativity should be clear. The nature of a would-be writer's or artist's ego ideal—how flexible it is, how realistic and attainable its standards—helps determine whether that artist will be able to do 20 or 60 disappointing drafts of a promising poem without giving up, survive rejection notices or bad reviews, or whether, after two drafts, if the work isn't yet clearly first rate, she will feel defeated and despair. One's ego ideal may value creative work per se and not absolutely require perfection or acclaim, in which case one has a better chance of being able to do such work and to bear the disappointments that come with it. If the ideals are unattainable and rigid, if perfection is not just hoped for but utterly required, the artist will be more likely to suffer disappointment and lowered self-esteem, even in the face of accomplishment.

A painter, upon being nominated for, but not awarded, a prestigious prize, felt that the nomination was worth little; only winning would have made him feel valued or loved. Having such expectations for himself didn't stop him from doing superb work, and in some ways clearly helped him, but the expectations did affect how he felt about himself and his place in the art world, and they made what another might have experienced as gratifying recognition feel painfully disappointing instead. In contrast, a poet told me he aspires to write great poems, checks his work against the highest achievement, but knows he's likely to fall short of what he aspires to, and can tolerate this, and keep going. For him, it seems, the internalized ideals are such that however much he longs to create great art, he still gets credit with himself, can value himself, for coming anywhere close. Greatness is the hope or ideal, but not the only standard, before which all else feels like failure. Thus the voice of the superego, depending on the nature and achievability of our internal values and ideals, will praise and love us for trying, or sigh disappointedly when the work, or the desired recognition, falls short, causing a corresponding plummet in self-esteem. This voice, like the several others I've considered, may help keep us going, discourage, or utterly defeat us.

There is also that potentially more objective voice, the ego's. It, more than the others, is likely to take the form of thoughts, opinions, value judgments, or assessments. The ego serves adaptation and defense, has at its disposal memory, judgment, reason, and the ability to test reality. It helps us mediate between our wishes and the requirements of both the inner and the outer worlds. As a result, it greatly influences our relationship to creative work. The ego can interfere if it judges such work to be a danger, and implement defenses against that work, or it can say, helpfully, reasonably, why stop now when you're working well? Or, perhaps, you should put this aside for a few days; your revision now seems to be making matters worse and this piece is worth protecting. Or, work here on rhythm or line breaks; those could be better. The ego plays an essential role in permitting us to do the work and can enlist all else on creativity's behalf—memory, the representational world, imagination, judgment, knowledge, as well as our ability usefully to regress. When we are in harmony with ourselves, this is apt to be the only voice we hear, after the muse. Where conflict occurs, those potentially problematic other voices described earlier begin also to speak. The conflict may be between our desires and those internal regulators of what we are allowed, between conflicting desires, opposing ideals—a wish to experiment and an internal value system that prefers conformance, safety—between wishes and needs, or wishes and the imagined requirements of others. How such conflicts manifest themselves has been illustrated throughout these chapters, with examples, in various instances, of where such conflicts may have their beginnings.

One other consideration belongs to this chapter on the sources and nature of those voices which sustain or berate us, and that is the nature of the artist's relationship to her art. Oremland (Bergmann, 1997, p. 192) suggests that this is an object relationship. I would agree. Our art is indeed an important other with whom we are internally and externally engaged. This important other may therefore treat us, or require that we treat it, in any of the complex ways that others, whom we love and may sometimes hate, also do.

Artists and writers often have such feelings toward their art as these:

> It/the gift will leave me if I. . . . It has left me because I. . . . It loves me. It doesn't love me. I have betrayed it. It asks too much of me. It will abandon me. It has chosen me. I happily submit to it. Why does it resist me? I don't deserve it. I must sacrifice all to it. It blesses, nurtures and sustains me. It torments me. It is forbidden, yet I can't be without it. I submit to it; I can't control it, I can only obey it. Without it, I am miserable, with it I am complete.

The art, also the muse, may be seducer, abandoner, beloved, or child to be protected and nurtured. It may be that without which life becomes empty and one feels alone. The relationship may be forbidden, dangerous. If the artist's relationship to his or her art is an object relationship, and the experience of many artists suggests that it is, then that object relationship is subject to the same hazards others are. We may turn from it to protect it from our love or hate, be so tormented as to be unable to function effectively within and need to destroy or subvert it, feel guilty about it, attacked by it, beloved and protected within it, or sustained by it. We may live with it in relative harmony, or passionate engagement. It may want a divorce. The *relationship* will be represented internally as others are and we may displace or project onto its representation any of the things that get displaced or projected onto any other, and with similar results. Our art may itself become one of those voices in our head which sustain or reproach, need to be placated or submitted to, are feared, hated, or loved.

The following contemporary poems, quoted in full, with which I close this chapter, along with other works of art which the reader may encounter, suggest that the artist's relationship to his or her art is indeed an object relationship. As such, it has great richness and complexity, the potential for trouble, the power to speak to us persuasively. It has, that is, the potential of such relationships, to guide us or to block our way.

A DWELLING

BRENDA HILLMAN

—And in the central valley,
people were dreaming of peaches.
Starlings ate the scalloped edges off new blossoms.
In the night orchards,
the dreamer walked over hot coals with the poems
and made creation seem effortless—there!

What do you fear in a poem?

(I fear the moment of excess, as in March,
when oxalis comes out all in one day.)

What do you fear in the poem?

(I fear that moment of withholding—
especially inside what I thought was free;
and I feared the poem was just like her,
that it would abandon me—)

THE CONDITIONS

LINDA GREGG

You will have to stand in the clearing and see
your arms glow near ferns and roots. Hear things
moving in the branches heavy with black green.
You will be silvery, knowing death could capture
you in that condition of yielding. You will be alarmed
by everything real, even moisture. She will not
tell you there is nothing to fear. You will come
to see her and she will blaze upon you, stun you
with the radiance of the feral world. But she cannot
take you up into herself whenever you desire,
as the world can. She is the other nature,
and sexual in a way that makes the intervening flesh
thin as paper. You will feel your bones getting
lighter. You will feel more and more at risk.
You will think her shining drains you of meaning,
but it is a journey you must take. And when the sun
returns, when you walk from the forest to your world,
you will have known the land where your spirit lives.
Will have diagrams drawn by creases on your body,
and maps on your palms that were also there. Now
you will recognize them as geography. You will know
an unkempt singing you will never hear without her.

Hard Wired

Jack Gilbert

He is shamelessly happy to feel the thing
inside him. He labors up through the pines
with firewood and goes back down again.
Winter on the way. Roses and blackberries
finished, and the iris gone before that.
The peas dead in the garden and the beans
almost done. His tomatoes are finally ripe.
The thing inside him like that, and will
come back. An old thing, a dangerous one.
Precious to him. He meets the raccoon often
in the dark and ends up throwing stones.
The raccoon gets behind a tree. Comes again,
cautious and fierce. It stops halfway.
They stand glaring in the faint starlight.

8

HELP AND HINDERANCE FROM THE OUTER WORLD

[N]o one myth can explain all
reality.(Glück, 1994, p. 107)

Several years ago, I was visiting primary schools in search of the right one for my son. At 4, he seemed to have artistic talent and I was determined to find a school that would nurture this in him. During one school visit, I watched the kindergarten class and teacher pleasantly interacting, then looked up. Above me, hanging from a clothesline, were six nearly identical versions of what I'd come to consider the s.k.p., or standard kindergarten painting: A-frame house, white picket fence, green tree with round, red apples and brown trunk, round yellow sun with prominent beams, one fluffy cloud.

Developmentalists no doubt have explanations for why, at this age, children may suddenly all paint alike, and choose such subject matter, but as I beheld this display, my mood grew bleak. I remembered being given clay in second grade. We began happily to play with it, then were told, "Now, make sombrero ashtrays." Grades were to be given, based on how sombrero- and ashtraylike the final products were. Mine resembled neither a sombrero nor an ashtray, nor anything else so much as the dismal mood the squelching, controlling command had evoked. These kindergarten paintings were evoking that mood in me again, though it was possible these had been done spontaneously, a thought which made me feel worse.

My response to the sombrero ashtrays and the s.k.p.'s probably wouldn't have been the universal one. No doubt I felt disheartened in part because of my own psychology or emotional state at the time. Had there been a future Brancusi or Henry Moore in my second grade class, a Picasso in this kindergarten one, he would likely have responded differently. He would have done something splendid that ignored or far surpassed what the teacher or group attempted to impose, or done the best sombrero ashtray ever, then gone home and made images and shapes that were his own. He—or she, if a future Louise Bourgeois or Mary Cassatt—would have managed to use the environments I found oppressive differently, as we each use our environments according to our psychological needs, our capacities, and fantasies, our unconscious ideas about what we deserve or are allowed. Some capitulate to environments that seem to invite defeat, others ignore such environments and go their own way. Some actively defy what the environment offers, or use it to make their own success, extracting from it what they need. I suspected my son wouldn't be constrained by whatever causes the predominance of s.k.p.'s, but could I be sure?

Shortly thereafter, my son, who hadn't come with me on that particular school visit but had on others, asked to paint. I was initially unsettled to see an A-frame house and white picket fence appear. His last paintings had resembled a vigorously swimming fish, "an upside-down chicken," and something so aswhirl it seemed to dance. I watched as he began happily to decorate the white picket fence with an ikat-like pattern of black and gray. "What's that?" I asked. "Bird crap," he answered with a grin. Whatever meanings his gesture may have had, we chose a school other than the ones I had been troubled by, a school where, among other advantages, the art was more diverse. And it happens that he is painting to this day.

To speak of help and hinderances to creativity from the outside world is to pose a partly specious but perhaps also useful distinction between outer and inner, between my focus here and my concerns in the previous chapter. We know that the inner world comes into existence largely through interactions with the outer one, that the outer world can only be seen by us through the filter of our inner life, that the so-called outer world will therefore be seen and responded to by different people differently. Also, children may begin to do conventional paintings because of internal processes associated with cognitive or psychosocial development, or age-appropriate desires to belong. It is not only in response to external pressures or failures of the environment to nurture creativity; it may not be the parents' or the teachers' fault. Still, it's helpful to consider some experiences as seeming largely to originate in the environment or external world, others as primarily expressions of the psychological or internal one, even if these distinctions are sometimes dubious and the interactions between the two are subtle, intricate. It's helpful, too, to recognize that environments influence us, including our capacities to be creative, even if they influence us in different ways.

We seem as human beings clearly to have a desire to create. Those who doubt this or consider this desire a pathological property belonging to a few, or who idealize it, need only watch 3-year-olds with paints or clay. They need only consider the earliest human dwellings and artifacts. There has been decorating, in all cultures, not only of bodies to enhance sexual attractiveness and thus help to insure survival, but of religious objects to placate gods. Pots and bowls, the walls of caves and other dwellings, currency, coins, and serving utensils have all been made to serve an aesthetic as well as a more strictly functional purpose. A great many things may support the desire to create or oppose it. True, some artists create even against, or perhaps because of, incomprehensible odds. The Russian poet, Irina Ratushinskaya (1989), while imprisoned in a Soviet camp for the crime of writing poetry, scratched poems with burnt match-sticks into bits of soap, memorized them so they wouldn't be found, leading to further punishment, then washed them away. The poems, subsequently copied onto scraps of paper and smuggled out of the prison, were later published. Miklós Radnóti (1992, Introduction) the Jewish Hungarian poet, forced into slave labor by the Nazis, wrote and dated his last poems while starving on the death march of 1944, during which he was finally murdered. These poems, five of them, were found a year and a half later in the pocket of his coat when his body was exhumed from a mass grave. A posthumously published collection of his work was reissued, to include these poems. Other people will be defeated by far less awful conditions, or will be unproductive despite, or perhaps in response to, apparently auspicious conditions and abundant support.

Our psychology helps to determine how an environment or a situation affects us and our creativity, as the cases of Ratushinskaya and Radnóti strikingly show. The conditions in which we find ourselves, the environments, will not, therefore, necessarily be decisive for whether we do creative work, as we may respond to those conditions or environments in different ways. Yet there are external factors which make creative work more difficult for many, just as there are factors which, for many, greatly increase their chances of being able to make art.

Many of these are beyond my expertise, and have been eloquently discussed by others. Virginia Woolf (1938, 1972) and Tillie Olsen (1984) for example, have written about obstacles to creative work as they especially exist or existed for women, as have many feminist critics. I have nothing to add to their analyses except to note that Olsen addressed the external obstacles to creativity as if they had no internal counterparts, and so limited her analysis of what silences writers. (Both Woolf and Olsen discussed economic factors, the impact of family demands and sexual roles, educational restrictions, the institutionalized prohibitions which become internalized.) Leader (1991), in his thorough study of writer's block, considers the experience of women in relationship to language, literature, and writing, and considers, for both sexes, the impact of cultural attitudes toward the written, as opposed to the spoken, word, and toward language in general. Rukeyser (1949/1996, pp. 7–60) has written of the problems posed by that resistance which exists within our culture to poetry itself, a resistance which she says is based on fear of "all imagination and the work that is closest to imagination" (p. 15).

That parents exert an important influence is obvious, though how that influence may express itself is not. Parents' conscious and unconscious feelings about their own and their children's creativity, about conflict and aggression, about the products and creations of the small child, will get registered by the child and influence his or her relationship to creative work. A respectful and encouraging attitude toward a child's creativity may certainly help that creativity to unfold. The film *"Maya Lin"* (Mock, 1994), about the then 21-year-old who designed the Vietnam War Memorial in Washington, and has gone on to design several other remarkable works, illustrates how her gift was nurtured by parents who held the arts, their daughter, and her talents in esteem. The lack of such support convinces some that they have no right, no gift. Others succeed despite the absence of such support, or at least its absence in their childhood homes. It is difficult, however, to imagine anyone succeeding who has had no external voice which offers such encouragement, no experience which suggests that her thoughts, imagination, and creations are of interest and value.

Teachers have played an essential part for many creative people, by believing in, challenging, and encouraging them. The six artists I interviewed (chapter 9) all talked about relationships with teachers as having been helpful, perhaps especially where parental attitudes were not. All of them suggested that their teachers' belief in them had helped them to believe in themselves. Each had had teachers, that is, who not only taught them skills, but had been identified with, *internalized* as a source of support.

Louise Glück (1994, p. 105), in her essay on studying as a young poet with Stanley Kunitz, describes the profound usefulness to her of the experience of being truly heard and of being spoken to truthfully about her work. She says of the mentor relationship, "When it goes well, something passes between these figures, a species of love, one of the very few whose limitations do not impose suffering." Richard Hugo (1979, p. 28), in his essay on Theodore Roethke as a teacher, says that for him, being introduced by Roethke to the work of Auden, Hopkins, Thomas, and Yeats, was "to be born."

Teachers also have the power, of course, to discourage or humiliate. Where a beginning writer or artist is vulnerable to self-doubt (and who isn't sometimes?), unkind responses, or poorly timed ones, can add to already existing internal voices of prohibition or doubt. So can discouragement of creative efforts by other authority figures. But one prolific poet, though he reported that he still feels angry decades later at the memory of an editor-critic who tried to dissuade him from writing poetry, used his anger at the discouraging words to fuel his determination to prove the critic wrong. This poet had reacted similarly to his parents' efforts to discourage him. He may be an exception, but he may be so in a way that many productive artists are—able to use even the most apparently disheartening experiences in the service of persistance and creativity, or able, perhaps, to ignore them.

Relevant also to a consideration of how the environment may help or hinder creativity are the availability of education, materials, and training, and of enough time, privacy, and safety, Radnóti and Ratushinskaya notwithstanding. Relevant in many instances are the circumstances of one's family and society, and whether, if in need, artists have access to financial assistance (through patrons, as in Renaissance Italy, the state as in the former Soviet Union and many European countries, or federal, state, or local grants in the United States). Relevant are the family's and the culture's ideas about what creativity is and who is creative; for example whether women or racial minorities may be creative. Also relevant, though none of these is relevant in each instance, are the culture's and the family's attitudes toward art, the process whereby it is made, and the people who make it or wish to do so.

The indifferent, ambivalent, or negative cultural attitudes toward art and artists that we encounter will complicate matters for us if they resonate with our own feelings about our work or with our own early experiences. We may feel marginalized or devalued in ways that correspond to our inner feelings about our worth and the worth of what we make. For the less conflicted, those same negative attitudes, or indifference, will probably seem more a cause for sadness, curiosity, exasperation, or a determination to try to educate others about the arts than for increased self-doubt or concern.

I've had several first-hand experiences, including in my professional milieu, and have had others reported to me, which seem to suggest a tendency, including among psychotherapists, to pathologize, trivialize, or disparage creative work and the people who do it. My examples are anecdotal but may suggest the presence of these attitudes in the culture at large where the more conflicted artist may find them troubling, especially if they underscore fears or fantasies of her own about the nature, source, and worth of her talent.

The belief that creativity, despite its pervasiveness among small children and throughout human cultures, is associated with pathology or is itself pathological, goes back at least to Plato, who spoke of the madness of poets. This attitude has been held, even nurtured, by various artistic movements, including Romanticism. Currently this attitude, or suggestions of it, have been known to turn up among some in the mental health professions. Writers and artists who express wariness about psychotherapy may not only be manifesting resistance; some of them have encountered, among therapists, a tendency to pathologize creativity and they fear, rightly, that to work with such a person would be detrimental to them. Of course they may hesitate also if they share the unfortunate but not rare belief that creativity and pathology are linked, and so fear that to "get better" will cost them their art.

One poet I saw in therapy was clearly startled and relieved when, after she had expressed these concerns, I asked her where she'd gotten the idea that her depression was the source of her art. Did she think that therapy could eliminate all unhappiness from her life? In the improbable event that it could, why did she think there'd be nothing else to write about? As we explored her fantasies about her creativity and its alleged relationship to psychopathology, she realized that though she held such views, she simultaneously knew, as each artist or writer with whom I've discussed the matter has known, and as Kubie (1958, p. 6), Loewald (1988), and others suggest, that psychopathology is more likely to get in the way of art than to be art's prerequisite or source. Not everyone, however, and certainly not every therapist, appears to recognize this.

I was asked to review a paper that had been submitted to a professional journal. The author had set out, as many mental health professionals do, to study the alleged relationship between psychiatric illness and creativity, in this case, traits that predispose to schizophrenia. This was a relationship the author's tone suggested that he fully expected to find. I questioned the basis for this implicit assumption, then raised other questions. The author had referred to the "antisocial nature of artists" as if this were a given. Did he mean the need, which people involved in creative work often have, for solitude, a need I did not believe justified his use of the term *antisocial*? Did he mean the tendency, which many artists have, to question or challenge societal values? If so, was *this* "antisocial"? Was he suggesting that creative people are more "antisocial," than the average citizen? According to Merriam-Webster, the term is defined as "contrary or hostile to the well-being of society . . . disliking the society of others"? If he were suggesting the latter, on what basis did he do so? Also, why the expectation that creative people would have traits in common with schizophrenics? It is true that both have greater access to what Freud called primary process thinking than many others do, but hadn't he noticed in what different ways, and with what different outcomes? Why, I wondered to myself, was he interested in searching for this particular relationship? Why are so many in the mental health field interested in doing this?

One comes across few studies of dentists and the various psychoses, or of farm workers and the psychoses. One encounters a great many, however, about artists and writers and the psychoses. Do artists truly have more mental illness? This has been alleged; has it been convincingly demonstrated? Or is there perhaps something which makes the alleged connection appealing, even compelling to researchers in the mental health professions and elsewhere?

I presented the paper from which this book evolved to an audience of therapists. The paper was followed by a discussion, by a colleague and fellow poet, of his experience writing a personally difficult and anxiety-provoking poem. His discussion illustrated several of the points I had made and expanded on these. When we invited questions from the audience, we were surprised, as were friends and colleagues who were present, by the clear pattern of questions and comments: What were we saying about creativity and the *psychoses*? (Nothing.) How are these related? (Are they?). Aren't artists sicker than most people? I tried silently to recall the last artist I'd read about who'd shot up a post office, robbed a bank, attacked a painting—someone else's—in a museum with a knife, or even shown up during my tenure working in the psychiatric emergency service. Depression, suicides I certainly could think of, but the rate is also high among dentists and police officers.

This trend in the questions and comments ended only at our firm request; we indicated that such questions pertained neither to our subject, nor to our area of expertise. We were discussing how anxiety and resistance can make creative work even more difficult than it inevitably already is, and not whether artists and writers are more likely to be psychotic than other people. We later presented our work to two other audiences of therapists, but emphasized to both at the start that our topic was *not* creativity and psychosis. One of these audiences nevertheless started to raise similar questions, but only briefly.

An accomplished poet told me about an analyst she'd seen who thought she wrote poems to compensate for not having a penis. This poet said that she was aware of envying men and even feeling, on a bad day, that perhaps they were superior beings. She hoped she'd be able to do something about these feelings; she considered them unhealthy. But she was certain she didn't write poems for the reason he had proposed and she seemed exasperated—I thought quite reasonably—with his simplistic view of her motivations for being an artist. This woman is a generally reliable reporter and observer; I had no reason to assume that her report was distorted.

I attended a talk by a psychiatrist on psychotherapy and Sylvia Plath. The speaker focused exclusively on Plath as patient and ultimately as suicide; it was basically a case presentation, though she hadn't been his patient. Had members of the audience been unaware that the "patient" was one of our great poets, they would not have learned so from him. Then why discuss Plath? Why not any other patient whose mental suffering seems temporarily eased by therapy but then suicides; whose early loss of a father scarred her? I had come hoping for insights into Plath's creative process and work, or the relationship between her therapy and her art. These were barely mentioned. The speaker showed no interest in her as an artist. Perhaps he wasn't even familiar with her art; there was no indication that he might be, only that he had studied her "case." Nor did he consider her art as something with which she may have tried to fend off her illness or illuminate her suffering. That she was a famous poet seemed irrelevant to the speaker though he had chosen one as his subject—or at least he had chosen as his subject a famous poet's psychopathology.

I have mentioned one researcher, one audience, one alleged comment by one psychoanalyst, one "case" presentation—all anecdotal and hardly evidence of a tendency in the field or in the culture at large. I am not suggesting on the basis of so little evidence that many therapists or analysts pathologize creativity. But perhaps some mental health professionals share with the culture a prejudice which sees artists and writers as odd, quirky, troubled, "maladjusted"; as more likely to be neurotic or psychotic than the population at large; as creating to compensate for greater deficits perhaps than others have in their lives. There is no doubt that some artists are troubled. We can all think of dramatic examples. But whether this population in general has a disproportionate amount of mental illness has not, to my knowledge, been determined. Nor does Rothenberg (1979, pp. 6–8), after his exhaustive study of creativity, seem to think it has been determined, though he acknowledges that the question is complex. If there are such findings, we have yet to ascertain what is causal, what coincidental, what a matter of how research may select facts or shape findings. Meanwhile, such attitudes, assumptions, or expectations do seem to exist in the culture and can be problematical for people already anxious about their creativity, perhaps especially if the attitudes correspond to the artist's concerns about the regressed states involved in creativity, or the uncertainty of the venture and outcome. Such attitudes can also be problematic if they prevent artists from seeking help with what may be in their way.

In addition to pathologizing creativity, many appear to trivialize it, to treat it as inconsequential, as something anyone can conjure up who gets a few weeks' sabbatical from "real" work. The following exchange was reported (Roorbach, 1995) at a party. A neurosurgeon, upon learning that the woman with whom she was speaking was a writer, told of a plan to take six weeks off that summer to write a novel. She had never written before, it seemed. The author replied that perhaps *she* would take six weeks off and perform neurosurgery. The physician said indignantly, "Don't be ridiculous. To do neurosurgery requires years of training." That writing a novel might also require some measure of training, experience, practice, and skill seemed not to have occurred to the surgeon. Such trivializing doesn't only occur in relationship to art and writing, of course. A pediatrician told me he'd taken a weekend workshop in family therapy and was now practicing it with/on his patients. An obstetrician-gynecologist told me of her plan to treat—that is, to treat psychotherapeutically—an adolescent with life-threatening anorexia nervosa. Similarly, people in therapy often report being asked by friends or relatives, "Why pay someone to listen? I'll do it for free?"

There are various other ways in which people appear to trivialize or be disrespectful of what is involved in creative work, though I don't know that in any of these instances such is their intent. When I've mentioned having work published, or giving a reading, several nonwriter friends and colleagues have suddenly informed me of their intent to write poetry, short stories, a novel. My typical experience is that they never mention this again. If asked about it later, they mumble that something came up, that they got too busy, as if writing poetry or a novel is something one does if one has some spare time. Several people have told me they are writing a book; when I ask about it, they explain that well, they haven't really started it yet but want to. Certainly books begin with ideas or wishes, but it's my impression that the people who write them are less inclined to talk about them before they're underway than are those who don't get past the "wouldn't it be nice" phase into the actual work. I can't imagine any of the people I have here alluded to casually announcing an intent to become fluent in Mandarin, take up skydiving, or become a Zen monk. They would, I think, assume that *these* activities require time, practice, discipline, perhaps courage, certainly stamina. They seem to assume, blithely, that writing does not. There are, of course, other ways to hear these comments, and that is not as a trivialization of the process, but as expressing a sudden wish, or reconnection with a wish, themselves to write.

I have heard people, in a modern art museum, before a Kandinsky or a Pollock, say that they, or their kid, could do as well with finger paints on the bathroom wall. Such comments express not only a lack of appreciation of the work, but a tendency to assume that anyone can do such paintings, that to be an artist is within the reach of everyone. Perhaps when we're 3 and fingerpainting, this is so; perhaps, along with having a disparaging tone, such comments suggest a belief that anyone could—and perhaps that everyone wants—to be an artist. Perhaps there is a relationship between the disparaging, cavalier attitudes I've alluded to and the innate desires of people to do creative work. It may be that the disparagement, the pathologizing, and trivializing of the creative person and process I've described, reveal envy.

When I had been writing poems for about a year, after a long silence, I told a friend who had known me as a therapist but not a writer, what I was doing. This normally supportive, thoughtful woman, herself a therapist, blurted out, "I've never understood why anyone would put all that work into trying to say things in as few words as possible." Those, I thought, are telegrams, not poems. Then she said, "What do you hope to get out of it? Fame and fortune?" I said no, I expected neither of those, and changed the subject. I hesitated after that to speak to her about my writing, though it was becoming an increasingly absorbing part of my life, and I considered her a friend. Months later, she confided that she had always wanted to paint or to write fiction.

I told a friend who asked what I'd been doing that I had just submitted five chapters and an outline of a book (this one) to a publisher and was awaiting word. He began immediately to speculate aloud and in some detail, about what would be involved in his developing some reports he had written for work into a book. He asked me how many pages were required, then mused about how many he had written in the past months and at what rate. He calculated how many more months he'd need at that rate to have the minimum pages. His sudden, or perhaps not so sudden, fantasy of a book supplanted my 40% written and fully outlined one, in the conversation, at least. This man had wanted to be a writer, but had given it up because he felt he knew, when still in college, that he wasn't talented enough. He loved the work he'd chosen instead and was successful at it, but in this exchange with me, the old fantasy or wish suddenly took over.

I told a friend who was in town and coming for dinner that evening that I had just received a book contract. She arrived for dinner and graciously presented me with a congratulations and a bottle of champagne. As we raised our glasses, presumably for a toast, she began suddenly to tell the story of *her* book contract. This turned out to have been an offer of a contract if she would write a book in an area she was researching. No contract had been signed and no book attempted. I drank my champagne feeling a bit let down at the brevity and fate of my toast. This woman had always imagined being a writer but acknowledged that she liked the idea of being one more than she did the effort involved.

I could cite other, more troubling examples of uncharacteristic (for them) reactions by friends and colleagues to my mentioning writing or publishing work. Though I've heard similar stories from others, I've considered that there *may* have been something in the way I presented my news which caused these people to react as they did, or that I may have projected envy of my own, or had unrelated reasons of my own to feel hurt or disappointed at their reactions. But I'm increasingly convinced that the reactions I've described, the pathologizing and trivializing of creativity, the dismissing of creative efforts and accomplishments, the sudden expressions of apparently competitive feelings suggest that envy of creative work is widespread, that many long to do it who do not; or think they want to do it, but hesitate to try.

Many manage to write, paint, or do other creative work unbothered by such reactions from others. But where there is sufficient self-doubt or guilt about doing creative work, or when the envy comes or is expected to come from dangerous quarters—a parent for example—such reactions can intensify the anxiety and guilt often associated with creative work and so make a difference in one's ability to do it.

One writer with whom I discussed the subject of envy and competition told me she had written intermittently since childhood but with long periods of being blocked. When, with the help of therapy, she resumed writing, she mentioned this to her mother, who, within a week, began to write herself. Months later, the daughter told her mother she'd had her first piece accepted for publication; within days, the mother signed up for a writing class. The mother, who had apparently always been overly involved in the daughter's accomplishments and particularly in her writing, had intermittently expressed an interest in writing herself, but had usually been engaged in other forms of creative expression, though none consistently.

The daughter, who was the more disciplined writer, proved the more successful one, but was troubled by the persistent sense that she was holding herself back. Over time, she realized that she was doing so because she felt guilty about surpassing her mother and about being enraged at her. The mother's behavior was problematical for the daughter because the daughter had conflicts about competing, and especially about letting herself win where she sensed that victory was important to the other. It seemed that to win subjected her to the risk of being further envied by a mother whose own psychology was such that she more easily experienced and expressed envy than she did her own ambitions and strivings. Had the daughter's psychology been different, she would have been able more freely to compete with and even to outdo her mother, or to consider the mother's strivings as a separate matter from her own. That is, the envy would have been less problematical for her.

The protagonist in the film *Mother* (Brooks, 1996) is a blocked writer whose second wife has just left him. He decides he'll better understand his problems with women if he goes "home" for a time and lives with his mother, a solution he chooses over psychotherapy or analysis. That his mother constantly disparages him is made apparent early in the film, as is his distress and bewilderment at this. His time back in her house, where he reconstructs and lives in his high school room, involves him in hilarious and painful interactions with her during which he patiently tries to figure out why she puts him down and is much closer to and more doting toward his insipid, conventional younger brother.

In time, the writer discovers that his mother has a secret; as a young woman, she wrote stories and essays, and was apparently talented. When he confronts her with his discovery, made while he was snooping through old papers in her house, she angrily refuses to talk to him about it. He presses her and learns that his father persuaded her to give up her writing when they married. He realizes suddenly that as her first-born, and as a writer himself, he represents to her the pain and anger over the sacrifice she made, the opportunities she forfeited. He confronts her with this, excitedly blurting out, "Don't you see? This is wonderful. Now we know why you hate me!" Freed up (no therapist, analyst or couch needed here), he leaves and almost immediately meets a woman who clearly can respect and admire him and his work; in their first chance encounter she declares that he is her favorite writer. The final scene shows someone at the computer—we're not certain at first which of the now two writers in the family it is—writing a story about the curative encounter between mother and son.

This mother's feelings about her son's writing haven't stopped him from doing it. The film clearly suggests, however, that her envy and resentment, at first unconsciously perceived by him, have constrained him in his art and in his life. Such envy on the part of parents whose creativity was similarly blocked, is often perceived by their children unconsciously and may serve to stop them in turn, or make them feel anxious and guilty about their aspirations. A problem which is at first external to the child, the feelings and attitudes of his parents, may get internalized over time in the course of their interactions, while also being shaped by the child's wishes, needs, and defensive strategies. The now internalized attitudes and feelings about creativity—the parent's creativity and the child's—then help to determine what the child will feel permitted or forbidden. Such envy may be an influential part of our relationships with the people who are most significant to us. If that is so, then envy sensed or imagined from others who are less significant to us may painfully echo these essential early relationships and be experienced as punishment. Or it may be perceived as a threat that others will reject or resent us if we pursue our creative or other interests.

We may also confront and internalize the tendency of others to romanticize or idealize the artist or her art. This can coexist with other tendencies I've mentioned and some I have not—to view creativity as a sign of pathology or madness, to envy artists, to disparage, be suspicious of or in awe of them, see them as flaky and weird, or noble and spiritual. Such idealization or romanticization can be helpful. It can make us feel justified in pursuing creative work despite the financial and other uncertainties, the doubts that people in our lives, and that we ourselves, may have about it. Idealization or romanticization can as easily serve to daunt or intimidate us, however, making us think that it is presumptuous to consider ourselves as painters or poets. We may feel that nothing we produce deserves to be considered art because it doesn't compare favorably with the works we studied in school that were held up as models of what a painting, novel, play, or poem should be. Such attitudes can be as problematical as the others, particularly if they correspond to standards and expectations of our own. If we need to produce what is perfect, as did the man (chapter 2) who hesitated to draw or paint because he wasn't sure he could produce great work, such attitudes can increase our anxiety, and our defenses. Or, if we are so constituted, they can be ignored, overcome, or even used to advantage.

Creative work may also be affected by attitudes not directly related to it. Women doing creative work often encounter difficulty because of the cultural and familial expectation that they be emotionally and otherwise available to others when needed. That is to say, relationships are considered to be women's top priority in ways not generally expected of men. Even where women are understood to have other obligations, they may encounter more pressure, and experience more conflict when those other obligations are to creative work. Families and friends may understand that a woman has to go teach a class or perform surgery or drive the bus, but may not understand if she goes into her study to write or her studio to paint, particularly if this is not her regularly paid work. Such expectations are often especially problematical because the artist may share, or feel too guilty and conflicted to oppose them.

A writer in therapy with me had been accepted by a writer's colony in another state. There, removed from other responsibilities, and with her material needs provided for, she was to have several weeks of privacy and quiet to write. She approached this opportunity eagerly, used the time productively, but had it interrupted a few weeks from the end of her planned stay by a call from relatives insisting that she return home to help with a family emergency. She complied. It was clear to her and to me that the problem could have been handled as well and more easily by other family members, but that they, because of either paid work or children, were considered to be busy while she was not. Sometime later, as she was preparing to attend another colony, a similar family situation began to arise. She was asked in advance whether, if needed, she could come home because the others "were busy," meaning apparently that they had jobs and children. She struggled with doubts about whether her writing was a legitimate activity which warranted her telling them that this time one of them would need to take care of the problem.

It was clear that her conflict was largely an internal one, between her commitment to writing and her feeling the need to be good, which in her family, for this daughter, at least, meant that she be compliant and available. Her conflict wasn't helped, however, by family attitudes which said in myriad ways that her writing was not a serious activity worth protecting from domestic or other demands, though other family members' jobs or responsibilities, were. Such attitudes may also have helped bring her conflict into being. The underlying assumptions seemed, in her family, but also in much of the culture, to be that responsibilities, especially for women, matter only when they are responsibilities to others.

This woman's situation involved a convergence of internal conflict and environmental pressure. But such pressure is exerted on and felt by many women artists, in a culture that tends to see women's first obligations as being to others. Moreover, it is a culture that tends not to respect or understand the creative process enough to accord it the time, solitude, and psychological space it requires.

Several women poets have mentioned to me that they have precisely such struggles between their inner doubts (their right to do or the rightness of their doing creative work) and pressures from an environment, external, but also internalized, which emphasizes their responsibilities and the importance of their being available to others. They may experience this strictly as a conflict between their wishes to make art and their love of their family, and not consider it also to be a function of internalized attitudes about their roles as women. I have heard men speak of conflicts about creative work, usually having to do with whether they have sufficient talent or success, but not about whether they have the right to the time, the privilege of trying.

An artist friend described being frequently interrupted at her work by her husband, the conductor of an orchestra. She would ask him not to interrupt her, but he continued to do so, often with minor questions and requests. Only when she asked him how he would feel if she barged in on an orchestra dress rehearsal with a trivial question did he, another artist, seem to realize that his interrupting was disrespectful of and damaging to her art. His apparent wish to have her available was being expressed in a way that undermined her, something she would not have done to him.

Certain friends, when we're trying to arrange to meet, inevitably ask whether I am free on one or the other of the two days that I have, for years, set aside to write. They seem not to forget when during the rest of my week I work and don't ever propose meeting during the blocks of time when I see patients or teach. Perhaps my writing days correspond to their freer or more flexible blocks of hours, and this is why the invitations seem always to be for times I set aside to write. Or perhaps, in their minds, when I am writing, I am not really working, but available. If I were to ask them about this possible implicit assumption, and it is one I struggle not to share with them, which is no doubt why it troubles me, I'm sure they would protest. Yet it continues to be the case that I'm asked if I am available on those two days and not during the rest of my scheduled work week.

That cultural attitude also may impinge which evaluates our efforts primarily or exclusively in terms of financial reward. By this criterion, work doesn't count unless we are well paid for it. The best poem by this system counts less than the worst TV commercial; a good novelist with little commercial success counts for less than the writer of popular romances. If we have internalized this view, especially unconsciously, those of us involved in the less lucrative arts, or those whose work is published less often or selling less well than that of peers, may add to the list of questions we pose ourselves, what is my work worth? We may find it difficult, particularly if we are conflicted about making art, not to answer in terms of what we are paid for it, or the number of works we have published or sold, even if these are not always the best criteria of worth in the arts.

Another attitudinal source of difficulty for some is the pressure to conform, and the tendency in the culture to be wary, critical, or dismissive of people who don't. Such pressure may be blatant or subtle. It can be brought to bear on the most harmlessly divergent forms of self-expression. Like the other attitudes I've described, the pressure to conform is reacted to variously. Some ignore it, unbothered; others are stimulated by it to take creative or other action. Some feel hurt by, but able to work around it. Others find it damaging because for them, it sets off difficult emotional reactions when it comes into contact with their internal expectations and demands.

I was en route to a restaurant table with a poet friend whose work has received considerable praise. We passed a colleague of mine who clearly noticed my friend's slightly unconventional way of dressing and raised her eyebrows at me as if to say, "My, my." My friend's clothing was only very slightly offbeat and not in a conspicuous way. This unspoken encounter occurred in Berkeley where, during the present fashion era, my colleague must daily see people with sundry body piercings and tattoos, spiked orange or purple hair, studded leather dog collars and bustiers—forms of self-expression infinitely more dramatic and conspicuous than my friend's. Yet not only did the look seem to disapprove in a bemused way; it seemed to be shot at me as if I *certainly* would share her disapproval and bemusement.

I thought about the stunning poems this friend was writing and felt uneasy to see her so dismissed, and by a woman I knew to be a great admirer of the arts. Fortunately my friend neither saw the look nor would have cared much; she was intensely involved in explaining to me something she was working on in her new poems. But what message do such gestures of disapproval of even mildly, harmlessly divergent forms of behavior convey, especially to those seeking ways to express what they themselves may be frightened of or in doubt about or newly encountering in themselves?

A few such looks as my colleague shot across that room, unseen by my friend, could, if seen, make the more timid and inhibited preschooler hesitate to paint those wild and vivid things small children paint, the kindergartener quickly look to her left and to her right to see what is being done around her that such disapprovers might like better. If that hypothetical kindergartener had grown up in an environment which nurtured her individuality, respected her right to express herself in constructive and imaginative ways, and valued the arts, and if she were attempting to be an artist, such subtle messages about conformity might not get in her way. But had such a 5-year-old early learned that to be different is unacceptable to those whose love and approval she needs, that to stand out is to evoke hostility or dislike, and if defiance were not her style, such looks might make her anxious. They might cause her to seek to avoid such disapproval by better blending in and not calling attention to herself or her individuality. A culture that exerts such pressures routinely will not help the more conflicted creative people in it find ways to explore what is uniquely theirs.

A poet friend, when I said I was working on this chapter, told me that the things she finds problematical as an artist are all internal. Except, she added, for the difficulty negotiating the problem of time—how to be responsible at her job and in her important relationships while also allowing time for her art. Otherwise, she felt, such things as the attitudes of others didn't really matter. I thought that this is not the case equally for all of us and it certainly is not the case for any of us all the time. For some, perhaps many, the attitudes we encounter, especially the ones that are painful or disparaging for us, resound loudly in those interior rooms where we doubt ourselves already or our right to do the work. But the teacher who encourages us, the editor who loves our work when no one else is taking it, the friend who reads our drafts or comes to our exhibits or readings faithfully, may provide that one sustaining voice from without that we sometimes need if we are to keep going in the face of inner doubts, guilts, anxieties, and disappointments. Such voices can stand for a supportive version of the outer world, reaching us helpfully some place within, as the therapist's, analyst's, or supportive parent's voice may reach us.

9

SIX UNBLOCKED ARTISTS SPEAK

Creative work, because it is an anxiety-generating journey into un-chartered territory, is inevitably difficult. Valéry said, "Go into the self armed to the teeth" (McHugh, 1990). Many nonetheless manage to do such work and to do it well. Creative work is easily derailed, or at least complicated by psychological difficulties, as I have shown. Artists and writers, being human, have their share of such difficulties, yet they proceed in spite of this and not, I believe, because of it. Many work steadily, with often dazzling results. How do they manage it? I decided to ask them.

I developed a list of questions which I hoped would get at that "how," then contacted six widely published poets, most of whom have also received prestigious grants, won prizes and awards. Thus, each has demonstrated an ability to work despite whatever difficulties she or he might encounter in the process, and is considered by peers and others to be a serious and accomplished artist. I explained that I was interested in exploring how they manage to do creative work, given all that can interfere, and asked each if I might interview him or her for an hour to an hour and a half, in person or by phone. I offered to provide in advance a list of the questions I would ask and offered anonymity if they chose it, as well as a chance, after the interview, to review and revise the transcript, to indicate what I was at liberty to use. All six initially agreed; one later decided against being interviewed because of a concern at the moment that to talk about creative blocks, even if these were not the focus of my inter-view, might produce one. Three, at or after the interview, requested anonymity; two did not. I then added to my group of five poets a visual artist, because I was curious to see how similar or dissimilar the responses might be of someone who worked in a different me-dium. To protect the anonymity of the three who wished it, I decided to identify none of the six here.

I didn't consider this to be a formal research project and so did not feel constrained by the requirements a research project would

115

impose. I wanted simply to ask what, beyond their artistic gifts, had helped and what had hindered them, what they do when having difficulty writing or making art, how they understand creative blocks. I wanted to learn in what ways their responses to the difficulties I believed they, too, must sometimes face, differed from the responses of people who *may* be comparably talented, but are stopped or slowed in their creative work. I hoped also to learn from these productive and thoughtful artists more about my own relationship to writing poems.

The interviewees, two women and four men in their early forties to sixties, were diverse in many ways. Among their parents was an immigrant who did not read English and had a disdain for poetry; a prominent literary critic with a serious interest in poetry; a novelist and a composer who greatly valued the arts. There were parents who'd once wanted to do creative work, but hadn't done so, or who were, reportedly, "frustrated artists." Their families' reactions to the interviewees' creativity had included outright discouragement and disdain, confusingly mixed messages, and consistent, loving support. Their socioeconomic backgrounds ranged from modest circumstances to privileged and elite. One poet had, through parental divorce, gone from being the child of a middle-class family to being the child of a welfare mother. Educational backgrounds varied, too: One poet had dropped out of college, the others had M.F.A.'s or doctorates. One poet earned his living as a part-time white collar worker, others were college teachers, one a university English professor and literary critic. The visual artist had graduated from one of the nation's most respected art schools and ran a successful and demanding business as a ceramic designer.

The five poets had in common a high level of artistic achievement. They had published 34 books, several with prominent presses. Twenty-nine of the books were poetry, the rest fiction and literary criticism. In addition to grants from the National Endowment for the Arts and the Guggenheim Foundation, the poets had received or been nominated for various local, regional, and national honors, prizes, and awards, had work in respected anthologies, and had participated in distinguished readings. All five had taught or were presently teaching in highly regarded undergraduate and graduate writing programs and workshops. The visual artist, who made a living from ceramic designs and was also a painter, had work in private collections throughout the United States and Canada as well as in Japan, Brazil, and several European countries.

I first asked each of the six when she or he had begun writing or making art. The visual artist was drawing by age 21 months, an age remembered by family because "I was drawing with a number 2 pencil and I was wearing pajamas with feet in them; apparently the feet had stretched out . . . and I tripped and poked myself in the eye." One of the poets was telling his novelist mother made-up stories before he was old enough to write. "She would sit at the typewriter and type them out as I told them. Then she would give me the typed copy of the story. These were fictions, not poems. Mostly about animals." By age 14, he started to think of himself as a poet. Two of the poets started writing around age 8, one "seriously," the other "seriously" by age 14. Another started at 14, "out of my love for the poetry I read and heard in school." The late starter of the group, whose father had abandoned the family to welfare when the poet was an adolescent (i.e., at the time when the others were thinking of themselves as artists) didn't start writing until he was a junior in college.

Though all six said they had worked consistently, I asked if there were times when they couldn't write or make art, and if so, how they felt at such times. One poet told me that there were periods "early on when I was young and taking in lots of influences. . . . They weren't really me, but I was so impressed by other poets that I wanted to sound like them. It was hard to come out from under."

Another, who had started early and written steadily, said:

> I skipped high school. Mostly in high school, I kept journals, but that was it. The periods I'd consider infertile have more to do with not being satisfied with what I'm writing, not so much that nothing's coming out of the pencil, but that I don't like what's coming out. I'm hard on myself when it's not going well, very hard on myself. Maybe there are two varieties of writer's block, the kind when you're writing and the kind when you're not. I consider them both terrifying; I'd just rather be writing than not writing. I'd rather fail when I have a pen in my hand. Other writers would rather endure the silences than write badly.

A third said that once, during a period of depression, he'd been unable to write for six months, but that at other times, when there were silences, never again for as long as that one time, he was writing criticism instead or was at a point of uncertainty or transition in his poetry, "when I just felt that I didn't see where my poetry was going to go next in terms of subject matter or style." Of the silence during that period of depression, he said:

> I felt it was one aspect of everything that was going wrong. The other times, I tended to feel that the silence was the right thing to be happening then, though occasionally in such periods I've had worries that I would never write poetry again. I should say that I'm one who believes in writing less rather than writing more. I admire writers like T. S. Eliot who'd produce a rather small amount and each poem was a step forward spiritually and in terms of style.

A fourth reported having tried to write daily for 30 years, but added, "I haven't been writing every single day. I do have times when I can't write. A lot of the time I sit at my desk anyway and try not to do anything else. But I've had spells when I couldn't write, sometimes for months at a time." Asked how he felt during these intervals, he said, "Miserable. I feel as though my life's work is frustrated. I can't do what I'm here to do."

The fifth poet, who has written consistently over the last 31 years, said:

> There have been weeks, or a month at a time, when I haven't been able to write, but basically I've written fairly consistently. [When I asked about those weeks or a month at a time, he said that they'd been early in his writing life, that] without the daily writing my life seemed emptier, worth less; I was less in contact with myself and other people. In my 30's, whenever there would be even a short period of not writing, I'd feel lack, or absence, and an inadequacy. That probably stopped in my mid- to late thirties when I was more assured that I really was a writer even if there was a day when I had to go shopping instead. But in the beginning it was fraught with anxiety, I think in part because I became a writer so much by an act of will, which is to say that I didn't consider myself gifted—nor did other people when I first started writing—so I knew I had to work very hard to get there, and it was a long time before I would give myself any leeway or forgiveness.

The visual artist, too, had experienced times of being unable to work or of working but being dissatisfied with the results. She said:

> I think when I can't work it's because fear has taken over. It's fear of internal judgment. I start comparing myself to other people, or I think why do I bother, there's so much other stuff out there. Or, oh, look at all that good stuff. I'm no better than that. And that starts to erode my creativity. I do that to myself. I have all those inner obstacles.

The interviewees had responded to such difficulties in various ways. One, when unable to work early in his writing life:

> [W]ent to the dictionary and picked out 15 words at random and started to put them together in different ways, and that actually broke it. I realized that chance could be one's ally. It was surprising to me that words could be put into shape, order, like music. I had been trying to direct it too much. [Later he began to keep] little notebooks in which I jot down random things, phrases or things that occur to me, or images or a piece of grafitti, or things I overhear in the checkout line at the grocery. I jot them down with no order in mind. I find them extremely helpful because I can look through them when I have nothing else and can be caught by a line or a phrase, or music, which will want to be answered, to have a mate, and it keeps rolling from there, so I've found that accident can be an ally.

The poet who had written almost daily for 30 years, reported that when encountering difficulty, he has "done different things. Sometimes I make up a project. Even if I'm not doing it well, I'm doing it. At least I feel that I'm not idle. Those projects vary. I've written long narrative poems. I've written plays in verse. I've written series of poems. I've tackled formal challenges, I've done translations."

I told him I'd heard he encouraged a student not to believe in writer's block. He said:

I did that for pedagogic purposes. In this context, I believe in writer's block because I've had it. Not believing in it while you're having it on the other hand, can be useful. I've been stopped, and I've decided to write a poem every day. That can work. It has for me. It's a bit like keeping a dream journal. You may not remember your dreams at first, but you keep a dream journal and after a while you don't have time to write down all the dreams you remember. The way it works with writer's block, you say to yourself, what I'm going to do today is write a whole poem, and I'm going to do the same thing tomorrow, so I'd better get this one out of the way first. And you do that everyday. I've had good luck with that, sometimes. My odds are about as good that way as any way.

Another uses hypnosis, a process learned in psychotherapy:

[That has] given me my images, peculiar, but it's given me access to the randomness of the imagination and of language itself and how it's like the instability of matter, it's very unpredictable, what comes out of the mind, and even though you kind of know some of what goes into it, what comes out of it is astoundingly odd. Also I have some affirmations, ways of talking to myself. Like, all right, you don't know where you're going, you don't know what this next thing's going to be, but if you knew, you'd be bored, so why are you worrying about that? Just keep treading the—peddling the bike, and you'll be interested. This works and it doesn't. It (the doubt) comes up again two weeks later. It's not as if you ever get over that particular one. But I give myself little pep talks and that helps. Talking back to the problematic voice in one's head helps.

The poet who has written poetry, fiction, or essays almost daily for 31 years, said, "I try to push the difficulty and self-doubt aside. I try to recall the pleasure of what it's like to be writing." Of periods when the work was poor for two or three years at a time, he said:

You do a number of things. One is you continue trying to believe that it's good, and I'm not beyond that self-deception. And the other is to keep plugging and tearing it up, which is, I think a poem is done and then I'll look at it and I'll tear it open if at some point I understand that it's nowhere near what it needs to be to accomplish something, to move me, to get somewhere I've never been. So I try and work that stuff out *in the work itself,* I try to make the work large and to make doubt—well, if worst comes to worst, I become more solitary. I'll just work my way through it during that time.

I asked if he nonetheless keeps writing. "Yes," he said, "Absolutely."

The visual artist said:

When I'm stuck, the thing I'm always up against is do I just hunker down and do it, bust through it, or is that a time to take a break and go do something else, go to the movies, take a walk. Actually I am somebody who's not able to give myself that time. I have to sit here and do it. But, when I've decided I'm going to think about new ideas, I have this thing that I do, I have to go downtown. I have to have a tremendous amount of stimuli and I have to decide okay, I just look at everything. So I look at everything and I'm looking at it very differently from the way I did four days ago, prior to making my decision that I'm going to work. I become very preoccupied. For me, it's pattern, so I find it. So, now, look at your corduroy (the author's dress)! All of a sudden I'm focusing on: oh, you have all of these lines. Your sweater has lines and your dress has lines. There are lines in your ring. So then I'm very aware of all those different things. I love stripes. So, it's an easy thing for me to focus on those, but sometimes it's iron or grill work, or some sort of coloration on a wall, so it might seem like I'm just downtown, but it's a different thing. I feel very comforted when I'm in that place of discovering design and color.

Next I freak out, because I don't know what I'm going to do. Sometimes I just give myself parameters, like I'm going to hone in on colors that I want to work with and I limit it that way. Sometimes it's a pattern, sometimes it's playing with an idea, a simple little seed of an idea. I can come up with images very quickly and it's a good thing and a bad thing because it's something I can fall into too quickly. I think oh, I've come up with this and it looks pretty good and I can go with it or I can think, push it further. Sometimes I don't want to push myself. I tell myself oh, it works, it works. Then my husband (also an artist) comes along and he says, "That doesn't work," and I think, oh damn, he's right, and I knew it all along.

Okay, now here's a question back. Why do we think that being "stuck" is a bad thing? What if the "stuck" is what you need to experience in order to be creative? Being stuck, there's an assumption that there's no movement, nothing's happening, you're in trouble, but maybe it needs to be rephrased. Maybe being stuck is churning and activating and bubbling and growing. And maybe just choosing those words makes it a little easier to deal with. When we say that we're stuck, then there's something wrong with us, then we're not doing it the right way, or there's got to be a better way, or really creative people don't get stuck. But you are finding that everyone gets stuck, so maybe we *need* to have those moments of just not doing anything.

I asked the six how their creativity had been responded to,

whether it had been supported or not, early on by their parents and later by other important people in their lives. Who might have helped them to develop a belief in themselves and in their creativity? Where might those reassuring voices, that determination come from that each seemed able consistently to conjure, despite moments of fear and self-doubt? Were there common experiences that might help to explain why they could so effectively talk down or by-pass the doubts that each, somewhere in the interview, acknowledged encountering? In their early experience within their families and the response of those families to their creativity, the six varied considerably, though not in what they said about the importance of teachers and of friends, especially artist friends, in supporting them.

One of the most steadily prolific of the poets had experienced the least support for his art in his childhood home. He said:

> Well, my family. My mother couldn't read or write English and my father, who could, just wasn't interested. They tried to dissuade me, thought writing was a sign of mental illness, and that's why, for me, writing started out to be a secret activity. I wrote and didn't show it to anyone and certainly not my parents, or my friends who wouldn't have understood anyway. I think that to this day I feel very secretive about my work, that it's done at a layer that's below what goes on at the surface. When I started writing, I had to go against my family, they wanted me to go into the family business. My father thought poetry was an aberration.

In common with the others, this poet spoke of having been given important support and encouragement by teachers and later by friends, especially friends in the arts. "The first person who was supportive and encouraging was an English teacher who wrote. I wrote some poems with her in mind." The teacher showed her student's work to a literary critic friend, who was similarly encouraging.

> The second person who was encouraging was 15 years older than me. He was a blocked writer. I remember telling him how the more I wrote the more difficult it was because the material coming up was painful to deal with. He said, "Do you have a choice of doing anything else?" I realized he was right. He remained my friend, and was very supportive though he couldn't write himself. What he couldn't give to himself, he gave to me. He knew a lot; his support and encouragement were very important to me.

Another poet said that as a child:

> I was expected to be perfect, and that I found crushing and terrifying, and not helpful. I felt very judged by my parents for not being perfect. I had a heavy sense of judgment as a child. As a woman my purpose in

life was to be an adjunct to a life and not to be a life itself, and that was hard to break. I would say that my family of origin did their best, given their limitations, but there were devastating things that happened.

This poet found support elsewhere, however.

I've been most nurtured by a sense there was something in the universe that was behind it or in front of it that I needed to speak to or on behalf of. I wouldn't call it a god, I'd call it an animating spirit that wasn't human, a sense of a presence that's with me, that's what I wrote for. I had a very lonely childhood, I talked to myself a lot, I did a lot of solitary walking and talking out into things and whispering into, and that, the sense of a presence being with me and on my side that wasn't particularly available to other people was always there. So that's the main thing. *Who* nurtured me? My first teacher in college was a very nurturing presence. He used to tell me to go for the odd thing or the great thing in the imagination and not just what was fashionable. And that made a great impression on me as a writer. He tried to dissuade me from reading what seemed to me the thing to read that I wanted to sound like. He said no, read this, look at this, and he chucked something else at me, and I'm indebted to him. Also my M.F.A. was very helpful. And my husband has been the main force in my writing, and friends have been nurturing presences. Oh, my therapist, a great presence, has really helped with the production of these books.

Another poet said:

Everything we've been talking about in a way goes back to early family experiences. I came from a very literary family. My father was a famous scholar, well-known, brilliant, and formidable. All the arts were very much a presence around our household, so it was natural I wrote stories, composed music, and so on from before the age of 10. I think that my father, however, was a problematic influence for me as a writer because he was hypercritical. So I always heard about the few bad grades on my report card, even if they were in gym, rather than the good grades. Pretty much nothing was quite good enough. My father, I think, had a very ambivalent attitude toward my wanting to be a writer—this is my speculation—having to do with his having tried to be a poet as a young man, having published a few poems, and then decided he wasn't good enough, and given up on it.

This poet suggested that while his mother had "made common cause with my father as a critic and disciplinarian," she had also been a positive influence artistically. "I drew some of my more personal and inward artistic style from her. I have memories of her reading Greek myths to me and telling me dreams that she had had as a child." He said, too, that his mother's family had offered a more expressive, emotional example than his father's family had, and greatly influenced his art.

Like each of the others, he had found in teachers an important source of support. In response to a question about who had nurtured his creativity, he said:

> I had very good teachers, I think; in college I had three teachers, all of whom believed in me and were generous with me. I had circles of writers I felt common cause with, both in college and in graduate school, who have remained my closest friends. And I had (he names a famous and important poet with whom he studied), who was a more daunting example since he was much harder to please than my college teachers had been. But certainly his encouragement, even though it was measured, and above all his example, I think, were very nurturing to me, though it kept me in his shadow for many years.

Another of the poets, who "grew up in a bourgeois household with poetry in it," had received:

> Complicated and ambivalent nurturing from my mother, who made grandiose claims for who I was and what I could do, so that I had no real trust in the truth of her judgments. I was just a little boy genius. And that led me to be the kind of person who had no real sense of his accomplishments nor his value, always in a shadow doubting that anything I accomplished was real. But along with those feelings of inadequacy came a feeling of specialness, that I was somehow someone exceptional. I think I carried that with me through the times when I wasn't getting encouragement and it made me feel like, oh, *I'll show them I can do this.* And that confidence comes in part from my mother's nurturing, and also in part from my class position, which is that middle class belief that hard work brings success.

He, like the others, had gotten important support from teachers.

> My teachers, up through junior high school, really felt that I was a special child, that little boy genius I was talking about. That part reinforced my mother's feeling. A college writing teacher was the first person who gave me books to read, told me I might be able to do it, and also made writing an integral part of who I am. He wasn't a writer, but he was terrifically encouraging, mostly by telling me what I'd have to do, how I was getting better, by being rigorous and asking a lot of me. He was the first person who encouraged me to be a writer.

Another college teacher the poet went to during a crisis in his junior year, took an interest in the poet, and "encouraged me most to be a writer. He never had any doubts that I could be a writer." Also important was the support and influence of a writer and colleague in the poet's first teaching job who critiqued the poet's early poems. This interviewee had previously stopped writing poetry, though not fiction, for four years after a famous poet teacher told him he had no talent. He returned to poetry, however, and with the help of his colleague, gained sufficient confidence to begin submitting and publishing his poems.

The poet whose novelist mother had typed up his stories when he was a small child, and whose father was a composer, said:

> The most important nurturing of my creativity was my parents. My parents are both artists and I grew up in a household where art was thought of as a fundamentally important activity. When I started writing my parents shared my pleasure and enthusiasm. Seeing them do their work and seeing how respectful they were of mine helped me get started. It's hard for me to imagine how people get started without such receptivity and support early on. It's been so integral to my life. I have a lot of respect for people who decide on their own.
>
> I'd decided that I was going to be a poet and my graduate school teachers took this seriously. They recognized strengths in my work and confirmed them in a way that gave me more confidence and helped me dedicate myself. Another thing they did was to say where my work was not as good as it could be. They let me know that there was a long way to go. This was really helpful, too. To get either one of those without the other would have been less helpful.

This poet, like the others, spoke of the importance of friendships, especially with other artists. He said, "A lot of the sustenance of my work has been sharing work with friends, poets, sculptors, photographers, painters, musicians. To have friendships in the arts is very sustaining."

The visual artist said, "My family was very encouraging. My parents and family hold in high regard anybody in the arts so that was really good for me." This artist didn't believe that encouragement had been necessary, however. She reported an exchange with her sister in which her sister said their parents had particularly nurtured the artist's creativity, and that "made me feel like a science experiment." Their mother, she explained, had made crayons available to all her children; the artist had chosen to use them all the time. Even if encouragement, though welcome, hadn't been necessary because of her intense motivation to make art, she had indeed received it, not only from her family but from teachers in the local gallery where she had taken classes from ages 4 to 15, and in artschool.

What had helped or hindered their creativity? One poet said that doing work which had nothing to do with writing or literature helped "because when you leave there, you're done for the day." Envy had, at one time, been problematical for him, envy of:

> Other writers, past or contemporary, imagining the benefits they've had, the reputations. But there's a certain point I came to when I realized

envy of other people's experience is a waste. When I teach, I tell students, "It's true, Shakespeare and Sappho had experiences you've never had, but you've had experiences they didn't, and so that's what you need to have your work draw from." And when I saw that clearly, I realized my envy of them was misplaced. It was "the wrong wound."

In Joseph Heller's *Catch 22*, the narrator talks about the "wrong wound." He's flying a bomber over Germany in the Second World War, and the plane gets hit where the gunner is, and he rushes to him. They see blood from his shoulder and start cutting the jacket open. Then, when they're just about done bandaging his wound, they open his jacket, and suddenly his guts spill out. They've been working on the wrong wound. So I keep thinking of that. It was the wrong wound, the wrong problem I was concentrating on. Envy is totally misplaced and a lot of energy goes into it. I realized I was stuck with my own experience. No amount of envy was going to give me their experiences, their ability.

This poet provided several other instances of *deciding* not to be upset, diverted by, or preoccupied with that which was not productive or useful for his art and so suggested something else which has helped him and which I will consider in chapter 10. I refer to the role of character or personality in determining who persists in developing his or her art. Another poet said that the sense of envy

had been problematical. The sense that there's no point in doing my work because this other person is getting attention or that other person is getting this prize. This sort of crushing sense that you can't prove yourself ever enough to please the world is very hard. But the encouragement of friends helps. When that doesn't work and the sort of inner struggle kicks in, I remember that only I can write my poems and no one else can write them. And that I've written good stuff and I probably will again. Personal circumstances have helped. I come from a very privileged class, I'm white, middle class, and now upper middle class. It would be bullshit to say my life isn't privileged and that it isn't due to this privilege that I'm able to write. Conversely, I see myself as a working class mother and as a worker. I earn my living working very hard, so it's not a nineteenth century ideal of a privileged class, or a Bloomsbury sense of the middle class. Also, it's still a struggle for women to write.

One poet had been diagnosed as having obsessive compulsive disorder, which sometimes manifests itself with troubling obsessive ideas.

When I have that symptom, I feel that I cannot write from my true self, that what I write is somehow polluted by the state of mind I'm in and this is what caused the long period when I couldn't write out of severe depression. It was not so severe as to require being institutionalized or having suicidal thoughts, but severe enough from my point of view. There have been times when I've been subject to such obsessional ideas and have only been able to write in the interludes when I can be free of them. In a more general sense, what's gotten in my way as a writer? When I was younger, I wrote with a good deal of character armor on, I had trouble being straightforward as a writer, or letting out in an unguarded way things that came from a feelingful realm or a dream realm in myself. Therefore I always felt I was deficient in comparison to the poets I admired most who tended to be poets who did do that. And I think this is something that has dropped away with age. I feel that my greatest gain from my first book to now is being able to be my full self on the page. I've had a lot of experience with psychoanalysis and psychotherapy, and both therapy and meditation have played a considerable role in enabling me to write in a way simply from where I am, my emotional state, which doesn't mean that the writing comes out simple. It may come out as obscure and with as many implicit intellectual arguments as ever, but with less of a sense of a defensive persona intruding in speaking the poem.

The poet who had felt most supported and encouraged by his artist parents was alone in saying that he could think of no hindrances or sources of disappointment, nothing that had made it harder for him as a writer. He said he'd been "extraordinarily lucky," but added,

> The main thing that makes poetry difficult for me may be my awareness of how few people who try their whole lives do it well, as well as it needs to be done. Art is a very exacting activity and way of life. Poetry in particular is a very labor intensive, low yield undertaking. Most people who work at it don't do very much that's up to snuff. I feel that I have to keep working some hours every day. It's like a musical instrument. You want to maintain your fluency so you'll be ready when something comes along. You have to work at it all the time. It's hard to learn that and even after you learn it, it's hard to keep at it. It's something you have to do by yourself. Poetry. With relatively little acknowledgment.

He thought his temperament had been helpful.

> I like to be alone a good bit of the time. I like to sit by myself, and I do, for hours, every day. Also my family—I'm married and have three children—creates a lot of other responsibilities and demands on my time. I've always thought those have been more help than hinderance to me. I would feel paralyzed if poetry were the only thing in my life. My intimate connections with other people have an integrity quite apart from the kind of work I'm doing. I think that a poet needs that. I need that.
>   I'm stubborn and disciplined. Those qualities are a mixed bag, for a writer. My disposition is such that I can conceive of a project and then spend years finishing it. I may get discouraged, but I'm not going to stop. That's a mixed bag because there may be better things to do. This singularity of attention on one particular undertaking may not always be the most fruitful path. It's hard to tell. I don't think that an unwillingness to give up on writing is a disadvantage to a writer. An unwillingness

to give up on a particular project is a disadvantage if that project isn't the best thing to do.

The poet who hadn't written poems for four years but kept writing fiction after a teacher had been dismissive of the poems, said that he had, at times, felt wounded and discouraged when unkind things were said about his work, "whether it's in a review, or a friend, or another poet." How he deals with that "depends on how strong I'm feeling, it depends on who says it. Sometimes I get infuriated, sometimes I'm really wounded. Most of the time now it makes a much smaller impression on me. I think one advantage of getting older is you know a bit more of who you are and you also understand that writing is not a way to win love."

This poet stressed the role of social class. "I had opportunities and privileges having to do with being someone for whom being an artist was not impossible. There were models for it in my life and that has to do with social class." He described the loss, when he was 13 and his father left the family, of that economic and social privilege which had included "going to concerts, things like that." This experience, of privilege and its loss, "is one reason why, more than other writers, I really attribute a lot of who we are as artists to culture as well as to family.

> Without that early privilege I don't think I could have been a writer. I don't think I could have had the self-belief to be a writer. I never would have gone to college. I think also having a father who left me made being a writer easier because I didn't have to contend with his expectations of who I would be. Having him gone was also a hindrance in that I had a serious hurt and wound, but that impelled me in part to write, that I had some feelings that I could not express, that there was no one there to listen to them. Poet Rodney Jones says that everybody he knows who writes has at some point in their young lives felt themselves silenced, and that was really true for me. Also, it's always helpful in this culture to be a man. You can be assertive, ask for what you need without the complicated responses women receive.

The visual artist said:

> It's very difficult to constantly take risks in part because I make money off of my art and it's hard to have an audience and to realize that you have people who expect something, to have it look a certain way, and then be true to where I am, because where I am isn't necessarily where I'm going to be making money, so there's that balance. There are times when I do exactly what I like and it feels really good to me and I like what I've produced because it was a challenge and it was new and it was hard and I had to go through something to get the end result. There are times, too, when, oops, that didn't really work and nothing sold and then how do you deal with that?

As should be apparent, each of the six, despite decades of productivity and at least modest recognition as artists, experienced
voices of doubt and self-criticism. Some acknowledged disappointment, some anger and frustration, at not having been more ac-
claimed—"as famous as Clark Gable," as one poet put it. "Not
Rilke?" I asked. "No, Clark Gable." "There are no Oscars," said
another, "no dazzling moments when you're getting rewarded."
Each had, however, ways he or she coped with these various concom-
mitants of and potential impediments to creative work, ways which
apparently helped keep art and artist going. Each also spoke of a
deep trust in the process and of joy in the work.

One poet, in response to my asking if he had voices of self-
doubt and criticism in his head, said:

> Yeah. Today. I always live with that. I always feel, to varying degrees,
> that the work's not good enough. Those feelings can live side by side
> with feelings that at a certain point in my life, I'm writing very well,
> but the ultimate value of it, I never know, and I always live with that
> contingency, sometimes better and more comfortably, sometimes it's
> debilitating, sometimes it leaves me feeling dark and not very useful.

Asked what he does when voices of doubt are ascendant, he replied:

> Oh, I don't have any conscious strategies for how to handle it. I try to
> push it aside. I try to recall the pleasure of what it's like to be doing it.
> Writing is such a wonderful gift in spite of the fact that I've worked my
> ass off for it. It's such a wonderful gift to be able to sit and invent
> and to make connections with language that reflect on you and your
> relationships with other people. That's what ultimately nourishes me,
> the joy of that craft, and I know I won't get it every day and I might not
> for months at a time.
>
> The activity is just so wonderful. I don't understand people who
> say I only write because I have to. You don't have to. There's no gun
> pointed to your head demanding that you write. Whatever inner compul-
> sions you have, it can't be as large as the doing it, or you won't continue.
> It's a blessing, it's the closest thing that I come, or one of the two or
> three closest things that I come, to feeling religious, the sacredness of
> it. The spirit of that activity. It's marvelous. It has never failed me. I
> have failed it but it's never failed me. I've never had a question for a
> moment that this is what I love to be doing as often as I can do it.

In response to the same question, about whether he lives with
such voices, the poet who'd had the most unequivocal early encouragement and support, said, "Oh, yeah." Asked what he does with
those voices, he said:

> It's good sometimes to listen to voices of self-doubt and self-criticism.
> It's hard to write a good poem, so if you have a feeling that your poem

could be improved, you're probably right. On the other hand, especially in a first draft, but even in the event of revision, when you need to reenter a poem, you want to feel unimpeded. You want to connect. There's a kind of doubt that frustrates the connection. If you're starting to get onto something, to feel inspired, and there's a little nagging doubt that says, "Oh, this is hooey," you've got to set that aside and go with the inspiration. I always feel confident that the voice that says "hooey" will come back, but I'm not always confident that the inspiration will.

For me, it's not so much a question of ignoring the reservation as it is of focusing on the inkling of inspiration. I need to focus my attention on the source of the poem. I have a religious sense of this. I feel as though I don't know where poems come from. It's very mysterious. I hope my poems come from somewhere that is larger and more consequential than I am personally. I try to train my imagination to pay attention to things apart from myself. A lot of what is involved for me is setting aside self-referentiality. The voice that says to me, "Oh, you're going to look silly if you do that," is vanity. Turning aside from that and putting your mind on things larger than yourself is essential.

You don't want to take it (the voice that says "hooey") seriously at the wrong time. I revise a poem for years and years. That voice keeps coming back to me and I keep listening. I trust the conscious mind. The faculties of consciousness, in the world of poetry these days, are underrated. People forget that even dreams are conscious representations. I keep trying consciously to do what I can while trying intuitively to feel what works and what doesn't.

When I said that he seemed to be saying that he trusts both the conscious and the unconscious mind, he agreed and said:

My creative process depends on feeling free. I have to feel free to use the faculties of consciousness and free to go into something that I don't understand. Both. If I feel *hampered from doing either one of those things, the whole dynamic of a poem for me is not happening yet.* For me, conscious thinking is a helpmate to the unconscious. I can very often gain access to materials I'm not aware of by thinking my way into them consciously. I can't experience them fully without turning loose the reins of consciousness and letting the poem wander where it wants to go, but the reins help me get to the place where I can turn loose and discover something, where the wandering is more of an adventure.

Asked if there is anything else that helps him persist, he said, "I feel that it's important. Poetry is a fundamental human experience. The experience of consummate language seems to me invaluable. If I didn't believe that the art of poetry matters to other people, I would find it difficult to keep going."

One of the poets who'd spoken of anger at not having been more recognized said:

My reaction, rather than doubt or despair, or in reaction against doubt and despair, is *defiance.* You know, all those people who wouldn't give me recognition were either evil or stupid. I was going to triumph over them. And one of the ways I was going to triumph over them was by having a very original style, or sounding like no one else. I think, however, that for all my defiantness, I do have voices of doubt or self-criticism. The voices I have to deal with, other than the basically productive self-criticism that it's very good to have (that line isn't quite as it should be) tend to be of this sort: How does this really measure up, in terms of the great poets of the past? Are you not more famous than you are simply because it's a decadent democratic age when no one can recognize the old poetic virtues? Or is that just a rationalization and do you stand about where you should stand, at best another minor poet in terms of eternity. That's the kind of self-criticism. I simply live with it, I guess. I write what I have to write. I deal with it by simply writing the best poems that I can. I don't hit my head against a poem if it's not going well. In fact, I guess my self-dislike is easily triggered by writing down stuff I don't think is good or by just sitting and staring at the page.

What keeps him going? He said:

There may be a question of inherited stamina here. My father was a difficult person but he was a strong person. The people in my mother's family have a lot of energy. I suppose you could say that I had privilege as a white male growing up in a fairly elite university environment, but my privilege has been very double-edged in how it's affected my career. Of the inner things, I think that a lot of it has to do with the defiance and the determination going along with defiance that I developed as a child trying to exist, and not have my self annihilated, and feeling that writing for me was the way to exist, more absolutely. That would be, I think, the best answer I could give.

I have great faith that my poems will grow in the unconscious so I tend to leave them sitting around in the back of my mind. When I suddenly get a phrase that seems right, I will write for a while pretty much only as long as it still seems to be right. I use my critical writing so I have something I can do more mechanically that I can shift over to when the poetry isn't going well and then shift back from. Eliot said he thought it was good for poets to have to have a job because it kept them from thinking about the poems too much, and he said let the unconscious do its work. But of course it's not true for everyone.

Another poet said:

When I'm in those periods of being consumed by envy and self-doubt, if I just get back to work, I get so absorbed in the work and the actual process of creation that it is its own reward, and it's a great joy, the process, even if it's full of failure. What's kept me going despite the self-doubt is my sense that the inner life is a process of self-discovery. That it comes into the poetry in this fresh way for each individual is a tremendous joy to me. You have to discover the god through inner exploration and the writing helps you do that. It's tremendously vitalizing to me to know that exists, that you're finally never able to complete your task, that you have endless amounts of work on this.

The poet who'd had the least support in childhood for his creativity told me he experienced:

> Doubt, sometimes. Self-criticism, yes, sometimes. But that's to be expected. In fact, they could be used as a positive too, because at least you're questioning what you have assumed. Maybe feelings of doubt and self-criticism mean you've reached a point where you need to change the way you think about your work. They can be a way of telling yourself what you won't settle for. You have no other choice. I mean what choice is there? What alternatives are there? For me, writing has always been like serious play. At first when I was a lot younger, it was very serious, and no play whatsoever, but over the years, it's become much more, the emphasis has been on play, serious play, a kind of dark joy. It's both. It's dark, but it's also very joyful. And if you've chosen to do something, of course there are going to be times when you hesitate, you're doubtful, but that could be the pause before the next step. And also, if you realize that you've done a certain kind of work all along and then you're hit by doubt, well, maybe you want to make another leap. There's really nothing standing in your way, basically.
>
> I think at the root of any art, there's a sense of despair—time's going to end. But when you do start working, then you're filled with a kind of joy, because you feel as if you're collaborating in the moment of creation, and the desperation, the despair, are left behind, and you're writing on this crest of joy. You discover new possibilities, new perceptions to propel. Then it's a matter not that you don't have enough material, but that you have too much. Then you have to start choosing. You discover material is anywhere. If you concentrate on any one thing, you can spend a lifetime exploring that. It's just endless. So you have to narrow and focus your choices. And in doing so, you create a form of language, which is a form of life.
>
> Art uses you, rather than the other way around. The words choose you, if you're attentive enough. Then your material and subject matter come to you, though you can't make conditions on it. There's a certain amount of *trust*, I suppose, that there is something out there and if you make room for it, then there's more, and there's a certain affirmation in that, although you started out from a deep despair.

The visual artist spoke of the difficulty of self-doubts, of "the things I tell myself to tear myself down and people always seem better than I am." She described getting past these by "sheer will and a fear of not paying the mortgage."

> I have to find that safe place that's within me alone. And I have to get to that real creative place. And there are things I do to prepare myself. I allow myself a bit more space. I say okay, you're not going to do this right now. Even though I know it would be better if I started to design right now. This isn't my most creative time of year, the winter. I have to force it. I'm just trying to have faith that I've done it before (design) and I'm going to do it again.
>
> What happens to me is I make something and I'm not happy. Time goes by and I look at it and I think, Oh my God, how did I do that!

When I'm in a new stuck place, I look back at whatever I did. I don't remember being stuck, I just look back and I think where did that come from? How did I think of that? I can't think of that now. It's like looking at photos of yourself. I think women do this more than men. I was looking at photos of myself when I got married, only two years ago, and I thought, oh, my God, I really looked good! But at that time, I didn't think I looked good. I would have looked at a photo from five years before that and thought, oh, my god, what was I thinking. I looked really good. It's very similar. And it's a weird thing. I don't think it's very healthy. And then there's complacency. You can enjoy where you are and feel good about what you've created, or feel like it's just too familiar and time to push yourself further.

I asked how these artists think about creative blocks, what they think such blocks are, and what causes them. I will describe their responses here, resist the temptation to discuss the many other intriguing topics which came up, and save for my final chapter a consideration of how the character or personality traits they described or otherwise revealed have helped them to work despite the difficulties which as artists they inevitably encounter. I asked them about blocks not because I believe they have them, despite the transient experiences they described of feeling stuck. I asked because I thought their perspective on the question would be interesting and because five of them teach and so have experience, of a different sort from my own, working with the struggles of others.

One poet thought that perhaps the person who is blocked "reveres someone or something too much and tries to adhere too closely to it—another writer, a tradition." He said, "When you're curious, you're more receptive. And strange things begin to happen. There's a kind of buoyancy. Curiosity really means you don't know what's at the end, whereas someone with a block probably has an end in mind, and that end may just not be feasible. So I'd encourage disturbance of the given. Creativity comes out of an unsettling confusion."

Another said:

Sometimes good writers can't write well because they haven't found their way to the language that will help them, or the language hasn't found them, rather. I usually just tell writers at conferences who feel blocked to write the poem that's in front of the poem, you know, whatever is stalling them, sitting in the way of the one they think they need to write. Write that one first. That one doesn't count. So they can feel that's out of the way. And if they can do that, they can usually get through to the next stage.

The poet whose solution to writer's block is to write a poem each day, said of writer's block:

What it feels like happens to me is disconnection. It feels as if I'm disconnecting with the sources of poetry. I could say in psychodynamic terms that art depends on primary process, that in writer's block, my superego has defeated my id. For me, almost always, the feeling involves, I want to say, contempt for myself. That's a little strong. Doubt is not strong enough, though. It's a fundamental devaluation of myself that makes this disconnection happen. My disconnection is a disconnection from the world as well. If you cease to be a part of the world, if your poems cease to be connected with what matters in the world, it becomes impossible to write them. I have to feel connected to the reader, too.

Of his creative writing students, another poet said:

Those who have difficulty have generally been silenced by somebody in their family, a parent, who has given them some feeling about what they're able to do, who they are, or else they have very difficult material that they don't understand but they know is dangerous and they're afraid to do it and so they won't. I think doubt, self-doubt, stops them from being fully themselves, and part of my job is to let them know we all have things to say.

He spoke also of people who think they want to be writers because they like the *idea* of it but don't really like to write.

Also, there are people who are depressed or stalled. I don't think there's any single reason why. I think a lot of people who "have writer's block" have it because they don't have concentrated, long periods of time to write. When they sit down once a week to write and feel like, oh, shit, I can't do it, I must be blocked, you're not blocked. You haven't had enough time. As a writer, you need time to stare out the window, to play with your computer. Today I was painting clapboards. There's a whole bunch of stuff you have to be able to do to release the will. If you don't have that time, all the rest of it's not going to come.

Clearly many experiences and qualities contribute to the ability of these artists to persist and be effective despite sometimes feeling stuck, fearful, or anxious, to persist despite their "Watchers at the Gate," those sometimes pernicious voices of doubt and self-criticism. Many things, no doubt, contribute also to their ability to know, as the visual artist reminds us, that "stuckness" may sometimes instead be fallow silence. They have learned, each according to his or her own process, how to persist in the face of difficulty, and how, also, to listen to the silence, to trust it, so they are not stopped or daunted.

10

CONCLUSIONS

I began by asking what makes creative work so difficult, then what helps and what hinders it, and finally what makes such work possible. Revisiting these questions after having considered them in relationship to clinical theory and practice, personal experience, observations of others, and the interviews, I propose that we distinguish *three orders of difficulty,* though these can and do overlap.

The first order of difficulty is one which all artists know and the six interviewees described. Creative work *is* difficult because it mobilizes anxiety. It requires us to enter emotionally charged territory and when we do, we don't know what we will find or what will happen as a result. The process confronts us with the possibility of change, of discovery, and calls into question what we thought we knew or were. Creative work is *inherently, inevitably difficult.* It makes us anxious and calls forth those notorious Watchers at the Gate because to do it we must give up rational, conscious control and forego certainty, risk and face many failures, pursue thoughts and perceptions which may unsettle both us and others. If we avoid this anxiety and risk little, what we create will lack depth and truthfulness, emotional power. This anxiety announces and accompanies our compelling unconscious themes, and these, in part, motivate the work. The anxiety is essential; it is not pathological. Without confronting and being able to tolerate it, we neither create what is significant for us and others, nor experience the joy the six artists described.

The interviewees all acknowledged this first order of difficulty and had ways of coping with it. They spoke of "making friends with despair," ".working it out in the work" itself, steadily reassuring themselves in the face of the anxiety, deciding, when stuck, to write a poem a day. They were able to persist in the face of this first order of difficulty because they had found ways to reassure themselves, and to create a structure which itself reassured, as the structure of

psychotherapy or psychoanalysis does, by helping to contain the anxiety which the process evokes. The capacity to manage this first order
of difficulty by calling upon one's sustaining internal voices, or objects (chapter 7), and by creating a container (chapter 6) for the
anxiety within the work itself, is essential if one is to make art, and
is apparent in each of the artists with whom I spoke.

The second order of difficulty is the one that may occur if, after
we experience the first order of difficulty, we become anxious about
or frightened *of the feelings, the experience of regression, or of the creative
process itself.* We respond not as the interviewees did, to the states of
mind which creativity requires as natural, necessary, and worth going
through, even if they make us anxious. We instead experience them
as frightening, even dangerous. The anxiety and excitement associated with creative work or the regression (chapter 4) may themselves
feel intolerable and evoke more anxiety. The uncertainty, the giving
up of control, the intense feelings of all sorts that are involved, or
those sometimes astonishing moments of inspiration, of access to
unconscious content which creative work affords—all may feel intolerable at times. The intensity of the feelings and fantasies evoked by
the work may cause us, painfully, to shift between psychological states
in a way that frightens us. We may, for example, approach the work
as separate beings, able to think about and symbolize our experience,
recognize our separateness, and bear the inherent pain, the sense
of loss. We may then begin, suddenly, to feel merged with others,
or with the work, unable to observe our experience, symbolize it,
and cope with the accompanying anxiety. Or we may, through the
work, shift from feeling merged to feeling our separateness and the
attendant sense of loneliness and loss. If our capacity to bear such
shifts is limited and the work requires them, if we have difficulty
tolerating anxiety, strong or regressive feelings, including excited
ones, we may need to avoid the work, or do it only sporadically,
retreating when we find it difficult. In some instances, where the
sustaining inner voices are insufficient and the work itself does not
serve to contain the anxiety, artists, like others, may resort to problematical means of attempting to cope with it, like abusing drugs
or alcohol.

This second order of difficulty is a frequent deterrant to creative
work, though if we encounter it early on, because of inexperience,
and then persist, we may find, as the six interviewees apparently did,
that such difficulty can decrease as we learn about the creative process and our relationship to it. Even people who are experienced,
however, may occasionally encounter this order of difficulty, especially if feeling vulnerable or approaching a deeper, more personally
charged piece of work. If this order of difficulty doesn't ease over

time, if it presents itself often, rather than in response only to particular situations or content, however, it may be part of a more general fear of strong feelings, of regression, or of giving up control. It may be suggestive of early developmental difficulties, or of traumas that increase our proneness to anxiety. Alternatively, it may prove part of a neurotic conflict. The second order of difficulty may overlap with the third, with which it shares a border often crossed.

The woman (chapter 4) who feared being lost in "the fog" that seemed to engulf her when she came close to remembering intense longings from childhood, and to engulf her again the one time she drafted a short story, was encountering this second order of difficulty. So was the therapist painter (chapter 1) who became too anxious to paint after realizing that a painting she had done revealed her unconscious knowledge of her cancer. The first woman experienced intense, and for her frightening, regressed feelings. Both women gained access to something previously unconscious. One did so through her therapy and her attempt to write, the other through her painting. Both then became frightened, too frightened, at least for the moment, to proceed. Many people, upon encountering the first order of difficulty, especially if unfamiliar with or especially vulnerable to it, find themselves facing the second and are similarly stopped, briefly or interminably, from discovering what they have to say as well as the nature and extent of their talent. If they stop the work or persist erratically, retreating when the anxiety becomes intense, it becomes impossible to say whether a lack of talent, or a limited talent, or something else altogether, distinguishes them from those who continue to work.

Even the most productive artist is probably acquainted with the second order of difficulty and has ways of coping with it. Supportive friendships among artists seem to be one. The interviewees, in emphasizing the importance of friendships in the arts, may be suggesting that one benefit of these friendships is the understanding of, patience with, and support for such feelings and states that artists often provide each other, especially when our sustaining inner voices seem to have gone off the air. Certainly, good teachers in the arts help also in this way, which is one reason our mentors are so often loved. The interviewees suggested that they were helped, too, in dealing with such first and second orders of difficulty by strategies like staying at the desk even through periods when little is forthcoming, and giving themselves assignments. In such ways do we presumably discover over time that anxiety and bad work are sometimes inevitable and, if not allowed to stop us, are often followed by something good. Finding this repeatedly to be the case helps us learn to deal with both the first and the second order difficulties. Such approaches reduce the likelihood that our important work will be avoided or that we will sit feeling anxious until anxiety becomes panic, or despair.

There are other sources of help with the second order of difficulty in addition to actual friends or teachers, and these are no doubt useful with the first order as well. One interviewee, in a passage I did not quote, described identifying several *imagined* composite or representative readers and addressing these, albeit not explicitly, in her poems. Such a strategy may serve this poet and her poems in many ways: by conjuring imagined others as potential supports in the face of anxiety, as well as by calling forth presences the poet can dramatically address, argue with, or confront. Insofar as such presences help us when we feel fearful or overwhelmed, they resemble those comforting, protective others called up in the traumatic situations I referred to in chapter 4, when a terrified toddler recited nursery rhymes, a boy sang to himself, a young man kept hearing in his head what turned out to be a fragment of a lullaby. The interviewee with her composite readers may, that is, be imagining, including unconsciously, certain others as a way to steady herself when anxious, as well as to establish a poem's tone or voice. Such strategies can be useful with the first and second orders of difficulty, as experienced artists seem intuitively to know.

The third order of difficulty comes from conflict, generally neurotic conflict, about doing the work, good work, or any work, because of what doing the work unconsciously stands for, or where it is imagined to lead. Such difficulty is generally manifested by resistance, as I've shown in many clinical and other examples. The second order of difficulty, which can also mobilize resistances, seems generally to be associated with fears of loss of boundaries or anxiety about separateness—being overwhelmed, abandoned, or merged. But the third seems, in my clinical and personal experience, to be associated with guilt. The guilt may, as we have seen, be about separateness, or about autonomous, exhibitionistic, aggressive, ambitious, competitive or erotic wishes.

The three orders of difficulty aren't entirely discrete. We may, through psychotherapy or analysis, stop feeling guilty about doing creative work, then confront our fears of the feelings the work evokes, or the surrender of rational control it often requires.

We may experience the different orders at different times. We may do well with the anxiety and excitement inherent in the work, then do less well because of something in our present emotional state or because in the work we approach more psychologically dangerous ground. We may, for example, do our work despite the inevitable, inherent anxieties, then develop a neurotic conflict, and feel too guilty or anxious to proceed. If this occurred only with unproved artists, one might imagine that the blocked simply lack talent. Some, no doubt, do. But consider writers of the stature of Melville, Coleridge, Tillie Olsen, and Henry Roth, each of whom coped with the inevitable first-order difficulties, produced important work, then encountered what appear to have been neurotic difficulties, perhaps about success, which led to years, for some, decades, of silence.

A successful sculptor I met at a party while writing this chapter said that even when the work isn't going well, he persists. I asked what he thinks enables him to do this. He said he does it because he has learned that such phases, though they make him miserable, are an inevitable part of the process. Only if he persists in spite of them will he get to whatever good work is ahead, to whatever, as he described it, feels true beyond taste or individual vision. Only if he persists will he experience those moments of intense pleasure that are his when the work is going well. It is those moments, he said, that he lives for, despite having much else in his life that matters to him.

This sculptor, like the six interviewees and indeed any artist who continues to be productive, presumably has fewer third-order difficulties, or neurotic conflicts *about making art* and presumably about experiencing excitement, pleasure, and ambition within the chosen sphere. Such artists are not so conflicted about gratifying their curiosity about their medium or materials, or about where the process might lead, or about their *relationship to and with the work,* that they become blocked. They don't feel too guilty about the rich emotional rewards they get from doing the work to go forward, or about working hard enough (and often alone enough) to reap such rewards. They therefore have fewer or at least less tenacious versions of the attendant resistances I have described than blocked artists do, though this doesn't necessarily mean that productive artists are less neurotic or conflicted in other ways.

The interviewees and the sculptor at the party do face the first and possibly also some second order difficulties. They are better able to cope with these, however, than many others are, in part because of having certain traits of temperament and/or character. By temperament, I mean those innate qualities which help to determine how we interact with our early environment and whether we can extract from it what we need. (Our success or failure here of course depends in large part on the "fit" between our temperament and the nature of that early environment.) Such qualities or traits include sensitivity to sensory stimuli, response (whether welcoming or resistant) to new experience, ease or difficulty in being soothed or comforted, ability to accept substitutes, responsivity to and ability to engage others, level of activity, and basic mood. By character I mean those enduring traits which make us recognizable to ourselves and to others, such as how flexible we are, or stubborn, persistent, easily discouraged or defeated, able to focus, how disciplined, and how able to tolerate frustration or delay.

The interviewees made clear that several such traits have helped them to keep working. These include their capacity to make use of the environment and to find in it sources of support and encouragement which could be internalized and called upon, when needed, for help. Important also were their strong motivation and persistence, their capacity to follow through in spite of frustration and doubt, their ability not to be defeated despite feeling anxious or uncertain. Helpful were the defiance and stamina of one, the tendency to feel anger rather than discouragement in the face of criticism, and to be playful and curious of another. Helpful were the capacities of all to commit themselves to the process and to find joy in the work. Such traits, along with the many attainments and capacities which result from relative success in negotiating the developmental stages, enabled these artists and writers to persist rather than be stopped by first and second order difficulties.

What does all this suggest about creative people in general? It does not suggest that to do creative work we must be exemplars of mental health, however one defines that elusive term. It does suggest that we need some measure of emotional health and strength—and probably also of support—if we are to proceed freely in the face of the three orders of difficulty, and that psychopathology does not engender but rather impedes art.

Not everyone who wants to make art is talented enough, motivated enough, or free enough of neurotic conflict in this area to do so. Not everyone has the requisite psychological capacities. But the degree of talent one has is often not apparent until one has worked in a given medium for years, and some of these capacities can be developed over time. Some of the conflicts can be resolved to free the captive muse so we can see what we are capable of once she arrives, and learn to welcome her. This all matters, as any stalled artist knows. To get stopped or to stop oneself before having a chance to find out what is possible causes a great many people unhappiness. They may try briefly, then give up, or try erratically but retreat when something important starts to happen. They may back off and always regret it. They may envy those who persist, but feel that it's somehow not in the cards for them, or is forbidden them, or would, for them, have been pointless or impossible. Perhaps. But how, if they stop working, will they know?

The blocked artist wanting to get unblocked may first need help in determining the nature of the problem. Locating ourselves or others in relationship to the three orders of difficulty can make clearer what interventions or strategies, if any, are required. Is it a matter of needing to arrange things so more time can be set aside for the work? Is the artist confronting conflicts about doing it? If so, how deep are these? Can they be resolved without professional help? Third order difficulties will, usually, require help from without. Second order difficulties may require such help as well, though an understanding of how the creative process works—with inevitable anxiety, unavoidable periods of so-called stuckness or doubt, and bad work—can itself help some people to proceed. The difficulties inherent in creative work can perhaps better be faced if we know that these are a natural, required part of the process and that there are ways they can be approached and befriended, or like the writer's pest in chapter 7, cornered for a time.

The sculptor who spoke of how and why he keeps working when the work isn't going well said that artschools should teach students the importance of persisting through dry spells (as opposed to useful, preparatory silences), and of practice. He was suggesting that the lonely, confused states which all artists experience might be more tolerable, or at least less likely to defeat so many, if those inevitable aspects of the process were more freely acknowledged and explained. Teachers should speak of their own bad drafts, dismal canvases, sculptural failures, perhaps even of their own anxieties, and of how these are part of a process that also yields results they are proud of, and for which they may be known. Writers are often helped in learning to live with the first order of difficulty by looking at the many drafts that other writers, including great writers, have had to do to get to their best work. If the fantasy is that one is either good or not good, and that this can be determined early on in each instance, that anxiety in the face of creative work means one shouldn't do it, then the fantasy itself becomes an obstacle, and adds to the anxiety we face when we face the canvas or the page.

Heraclitus said, "Character is fate" (Davenport, 1995, p. 165). The poet Frank Bidart has written, "What you love is your fate" (1990, pp. 14–15). What I have learned about creativity in working therapeutically with artists and writers, and from my own joys and miseries at the desk, convinces me that both Heraclitus' assertion and Bidart's are deeply true. Yet just as neurotic conflicts can be lessened or resolved, character is, in varying degrees, modifiable. We can learn to let it serve us and the process, to let our defiance, or stubbornness, or persistence serve, to learn ways to bolster what is timid in us or afraid, to make friends with despair, and to give our own particular Watcher at the Gate a name. What we love, on the other hand, we may not be able to change. We have some say, however, in whether we are true to or betray it and surely that's the choice we face when we find our muse enthralled.

REFERENCES

Bergmann, M. V. (1997). Creative work, work inhibitions, and their relation to internal objects. In C. W. Socarides & S. Kramer (Eds.), *Work and its inhibitions* (pp. 191–207). Madison, CT: International Universities Press.

Bidart, F. (1990). Guilty of dust. In *The western night: Collected poems 1965–90* (pp. 14–15). New York: Farrar, Straus & Giroux.

Bloom, H. (1973). *The anxiety of influence: A theory of poetry.* New York: Oxford University Press.

Brooks, A. (Director) (1996). *Mother.* A Scott Rudin Production. Paramount Pictures. An Albert Brooks Film.

Bruck, J. (1997). The Warren Wilson MFA program turns twenty. *AWP Chronicle, 29,* 21–24.

Calvino, I. (1981). *If on a winter's night a traveler* (G. Einaudi, trans.). New York: Harcourt, Brace, Jovanovitch. (Original publication 1979)

Davenport, G. (1995). Herakleitos. In *Seven Greeks: Translations* (p. 165). New York: New Directions.

Ehrenzwieg, A. (1967). *The hidden order of art.* Berkeley: University of California Press.

Eliot, T. S. (1958). *Four quartets.* London: Faber & Faber. (Original work published 1944)

Ellmann, R. (1982). *Biography of James Joyce.* New York: Oxford University Press. (Original work published 1959)

Fadiman, C., Ed. (1985). *The Little Brown book of anecdotes.* Boston: Little, Brown.

Gilbert, J. (1994). Hard wired. In *The great fires: Poems 1982–1992* (p. 45). New York: Knopf.

Glück, L. (1994). On Stanley Kunitz. In *Proofs and theories: Essays on poetry* (pp. 107–111). Hopewell, NJ: Ecco Press.

Godwin, G. (1995). Rituals and readiness. In *The writing life: National Book Award authors* (pp. 8–10). New York: Random House.

Golden, G. K. (1987). Creativity: An object relations perspective. *Clinical Social Work Journal, 15,* 214–222.

Greenacre, P. (1971). The childhood of the artist: Libidinal phase development and giftedness. In *Emotional growth* (Vol. 2, pp.

144

REFERENCES

485–486). New York: International Universities Press. (Original work published 1957)

Greenson, R. (1978). A dream while drowning. In *Explorations in psychoanalysis* (pp. 415–423). New York: International Universities Press.

Gregg, L. (1991). The conditions. In *Sacraments of desire* (p. 46). St. Paul, MN: Grey Wolf Press.

Hamer, F. (1995). *Psychoanalytic insights and poems: Parallels in their creation.* Panel Presentation, Spring Meeting, Division 39 of the American Psychological Association. New York.

Has, W. (Director). (1965). *The Saragosse manuscript.* Polish film. Subtitles.

Hass, R. (1984). Listening and making. In *Twentieth century pleasures* (pp. 113–117). New York: Ecco Press.

Herrnstein Smith, B. (1968). *Poetic closure: A study of how poems end.* Chicago: University of Chicago Press.

Hillman, B. (1992). A dwelling. In *Death Tractates* (p. 22). Middletown, CT: Wesleyan University Press.

Hirshfield, J. (1995). Facing the lion: The way of shadow and light in some twentieth century poems. *American Poetry Review, 15,* 7–15.

Hugo, R. (1979). *The triggering town: Lectures and essays on poetry and writing.* New York: W. W. Norton.

Kinnell, G. (1982). The bear. In *Selected poems* (p. 92). Boston: Houghton, Mifflin.

Kris, E. (1964). *Psychoanalytic explorations in art.* New York: Schocken Books.

Kubie, L. (1958). *Neurotic distortion of the creative process.* New York: Noonday Press/Farrar, Straus & Giroux.

Leader, Z. (1991). *Writer's block.* Baltimore: Johns Hopkins University Press.

Loewald, H. (1980a). The waning of the Oedipus complex. In *Papers on psychoanalysis* (pp. 384–404). New Haven, CT: Yale University Press.

Loewald, H. (1980b). Primary process, secondary process, and language. In *Papers on psychoanalysis* (pp. 178–206). New Haven, CT: Yale University Press.

Loeward, H. (1988). *Sublimation: Inquiries into theoretical psychoanalysis.* New Haven, CT: Yale University Press.

McDougall, J. (1991). Sexual identity, trauma and creativity. *Psychoanalytic Inquiry, 11,* 559–581.

McDougall, J. (1995), *The many faces of eros: A psychoanalytic exploration of human sexuality.* New York: W. W. Norton.

McHugh, H. (1990). *Lecture.* MFA program for writers. Warren Wilson College.

Milner, M. (aka Joanna Field). (1957). *On not being able to paint.* Los Angeles: Jeremy P. Tarcher.

Mock, F. L. (Director). (1994). *Maya Lin: A strong, clear vision.* A film.

Ogden, T. (1989). *The primitive edge of experience.* Northvale, NJ: Jason Aronson.

Olsen, T. (1984). *Silences.* New York: Dell.

Phillips, A. (1993). Looking at obstacles. In *On kissing, tickling, and being bored* (pp. 79–92). Cambridge, MA: Harvard University Press.

Pines, D. (1993). *A woman's unconscious uses of her body.* New Haven, CT: Yale University Press.

Pinsky, R. (1988). *Discussion.* Napa Valley Poetry Conference, Napa, California.

Radnóti, M. (1992). Introduction. In Z. Ozsváth & F. Turner (Trans.), *Foamy sky: The major poems of Miklós Radnóti* (pp. xiii–xiv). Princeton, NJ: Princeton University Press.

Ratushinskaya, I. (1989). Publisher's note. In *Pencil letter: Poems* (p. 9). New York: Knopf.

Rilke, R. M. (1985). Introduction by H. W. Petzet. In J. Agee (Trans.), *Letters on Cezanne.* New York: Fromm International. (Original work published 1961)

Roorbach, W. (1995). On apprenticeship. *Poets and writers, 23,* 21–23.

Rothenberg, A. (1979). *The emerging goddess: The creative process in art, science and other fields.* Chicago: University of Chicago Press.

Rukeyser, M. (1996). *The life of poetry.* Ashfield, MA: Paris Press. (Original work published 1949)

Sandler, J. & B. Rosenblatt (1962). The concept of the representational world. In *The Psychoanalytic study of the child, 17,* 128–145. New York: International Universities Press.

Schafer, R. (1958). Regression in the service of the ego. The relevance of a psychoanalytic concept for personality assessment. In *Assessment and Human Values,* ed. G. Lindzey (p. 123). New York: Rineholt.

Segal, H. (1991). *Dream, phantasy and art.* London: Tavistock/Routledge.

Settlage, C. (1989). The psychoanalytic theory and understanding of psychic development during the second and third years of life. In S. Greenspan & G. Pollock (Eds.), *The course of life, Vol. 2: Early childhood* (pp. 365–386). Madison, CT: International Universities Press. (Original work published 1980)

Shapiro, D. (1965). *Neurotic styles.* New York: Basic Books.

Stevens, W. (1990). The snow man. In H. Stevens (Ed.), *The palm at the end of the mind: Selected poems and a play.* New York: Vintage Books. (Original work published 1923)

Terr, L. C. (1984). Time and trauma. In *The psychoanalytic study of the child, 39*, 633–665. New Haven, CT: Yale University Press.

Winnicott, D. W. (1965). *The maturational processes and the facilitating environment.* New York: International Universities Press.

Winnicott, D. W. (1971a). Transitional objects and transitional phenomena. In *Playing and reality* (pp. 1–25). Harmondsworth, U.K.: Penguin Books. (Original work published 1951)

Winnicott, D. W. (1971b). The location of cultural experience. In *Playing and reality* (pp. 95–103). Harmondsworth, U.K.: Penguin Books.

Woolf, V. (1938). *Three guineas.* New York: Harcourt, Brace & World.

Woolf, V. (1972). *A room of one's own.* Harmondsworth, U.K.: Penguin Books. (Original work published 1925)

Yeats, W. B. (1979). Untitled poem. In P. Alt & R. K. Alspach (Eds.), *Variorum edition of the poems of W. B. Yeats.* New York: Macmillan. (Original work published 1940)

NAME INDEX

SUBJECT INDEX

DATE DUE

THE CAPTIVE
MUSE